INSIDE ART DECO

A Pictorial Tour of Deco Interiors from Their Origins to Today

Lucy D. Rosenfeld

Schiffer Publishing Ltd®

4880 Lower Valley Road, Atglen, PA 19310 USA

Library of Congress Cataloging-in-Publication Data

Rosenfeld, Lucy D., 1939-
  Inside art deco : a pictorial tour of deco interiors from their origins to today / Lucy D. Rosenfeld.
      p. cm.
  ISBN 0-7643-2275-3 (hardcover)
1. Decoration and ornament—Art deco. 2. Interior decoration—History—20th century. 3. Art deco. I. Title.

NK1986.A78R67 2005
709'.04'012—dc22
                            2005017517

Cover and book designed by Bruce Waters
Type set in Trajan Pro and Humanist Light

ISBN: 0-7643-2275-3
Printed in China

Published by Schiffer Publishing Ltd.
4880 Lower Valley Road
Atglen, PA 19310
Phone: (610) 593-1777; Fax: (610) 593-2002
E-mail: Info@schifferbooks.com

For the largest selection of fine reference books on this and related subjects, please visit our web
site at **www.schifferbooks.com**
We are always looking for people to write books on new and related subjects. If you have an idea
for a book please contact us at the above address.

This book may be purchased from the publisher.
Include $3.95 for shipping.
Please try your bookstore first.
You may write for a free catalog.

In Europe, Schiffer books are distributed by
Bushwood Books
6 Marksbury Ave.
Kew Gardens
Surrey TW9 4JF England
Phone: 44 (0) 20 8392-8585; Fax: 44 (0) 20 8392-9876
E-mail: info@bushwoodbooks.co.uk
Free postage in the U.K., Europe; air mail at cost.

CONTENTS

Today "Art Deco" is a well-known, much-loved term, loosely referring to architecture, interior design, and furniture of the period between the two World Wars. It is used to describe everything from the Chrysler Building in New York to high-styled interior décor, from streamlined architectural zig-zags to leaping gazelles on lighted glass walls. In fact, it wasn't until the 1960s that the name came to mean a particular—if eclectic—style of design. As these pages will demonstrate, the Art Deco idiom can be traced through almost a century of design, including the present time.

The term "Art Deco" does, of course, derive from the stunning exhibition in Paris in 1925, when the "Exposition des Arts Decoratifs et Industriels Modernes" opened. This sensational show brought what was known as "le style Moderne" to the public's attention. But, certainly the Deco style did not spring full-blown into the world. Modernism, including Cubism and the Bauhaus were already influential elements of aesthetic design, as were motifs of the industrial age and technological advance. The celebration and inclusion of exotic images from Russia, Asia, and Africa, and the use of symbols and the allegorical had already begun.

But in Paris in 1925 the new, sophisticated style brought many disparate elements together. It was a style made for luxury living in a new age. Despite its references to stark modern design, Deco became somewhat of an antidote to functionalism, a return to more ornate design of the previous century. As much a commercial as aesthetic exhibition, the new design Exposition succeeded far beyond expectations. Designers from all over the world came to Paris to see it, taking the new ideas home to their countries. (Art Deco buildings are still standing in Mexico, London, Australia, Brazil, and all over Europe and the United States; and objects from the 20s and 30s are in ever increasing demand world-wide.)

The influence of the Exposition was startling. Before long, the modern movement had affected everything from architecture to fabric and fashion. Deco design became a heady form of modernism, with its stylized and highly decorative take on both the grand and the intimate: towering skyscrapers and dramatic interiors, high-styled furniture and elegant windows and grillwork, glamorous steamships and sleek automobiles, stylized sculpture and mirrored walls. Paintings, sculpture, and crafts were integral to the Deco interior. Deco design was able to combine the glory of the past with the promise of the future. From its columns, geometric forms, and stylized figures echoing ancient Greece to its heady, lighted zigzags and exotic curves, Deco seemed to embody both tradition and innovation.

This era of modernism in design coincided with many social and economic developments in the United States. Americans seized on the new elements of style as a kind of national "vision," where the new design could bring together its many disparate peoples. It was seen as a style of art and architecture in harmony with the Machine Age. Images of industry, as well as new materials like plastic and chrome, emphasized this connection. And when the Great Depression struck, Deco designers turned to mass production, another realm in which the arts and industry could collaborate.

In fact, an American form of this modernist style suited the national taste. Americans wanted to be "modern," to embrace the 20th century. With its emphasis on energy and speed, the style fit well with the new era of mass transportation and industrialization. And Deco's eclectic nature allowed for vernacular and exotic stylization, upholding both the nation's nationalist instincts and its regionalism. Many Deco designs included Native American motifs, indigenous flower forms, and symbolic figures representing national ideals. As new buildings and new picture palaces in the modern style were built across the country, Deco became a symbol of American vigor and enthusiasm. What had begun as an up-scale design movement in Paris for the luxury market became, in the United States, a kind of populist aesthetic movement.

In the last few decades preservationists, architects, and designers have come to value the Deco style and idiom. Not only have Deco buildings been saved and renovated, but also elements of the style have increasingly attracted contemporary designers and architects. For Deco design has long signified chic elegance and grace, and more and more of its elements are being incorporated into contemporary work.

The following pictorial survey of the Deco interior traces the progression from European "moderne" to its American form, and then moves to the present day. For Art Deco is back, both as an historical style worth revitalizing in buildings across the nation, and as a new component of contemporary design and architecture. This is the pictorial story of where Deco came from, how it evolved in the United States, and how it is used today.

PART I

THE ORIGINS OF
ART DECO IN EUROPE

Art Deco, at first glance, may appear unfathomable as a style; it is filled with contradictions, a miscellany of symbols and design elements, and a wide mixture of media. No two Art Deco buildings or interiors look the same.

It is precisely this design depth that makes the Deco era so fascinating to architects, design enthusiasts, and collectors. For out of a great many origins and sources a coherent and very popular style did develop—one in which historical and exotic elements mixed with the newest and most modern. As a style of design, Art Deco absorbed the work of painters and sculptors and architects, scientific invention, and industrial design. And Deco itself spread into every aspect of the visual arts, from architecture and interior design to furniture, clothing, lighting, pottery, fabric, and theatrical sets.

Where did Art Deco come from? Why does it look so different from the styles it followed? Before the Art Deco phenomenon in America can be understood, it is necessary to look closely at the characteristics of European Art Deco. For the style did not spring full-blown into fashion. Its characteristics were the outgrowths of a number of contrasting styles that preceded it in interior design, the fine arts, industrial design, and a variety of exotic cultures. No design style—before or since—has drawn on such disparate origins at the same time. The following pages include some of the most influential design sources of European Art Deco, as it was introduced in Paris in 1925. These sources, as shown here, range from art to architecture, from exotic cultures and distant lands, to industrial inventions.

ART NOUVEAU

The curving, often parallel forms of Art Nouveau were, of course, major precursors of Art Deco throughout Europe. More than thirty years earlier, in the late 19th century, the sinuous, flower-like lines—or what is now described as "organic naturalism"—of Art Nouveau appeared in architecture and many other forms of design. Typical were the parallel curving stripes that snaked through the creations of Arthur Macmurdo in England, as seen in his title page for Wren's "City of Churches," and the decorative metalwork used in architecture by Victor Horta in Brusssels. He was particularly interested in the flowing lines that could be created with metal; his designs for architecture included, in addition to iron construction, elaborate ornamental railings and handles that epitomized Art Nouveau's decorative line.

Charles Rennie Mackintosh's brilliant designs in Scotland had wide influence, for it was he who brought every element of a room into harmony. His vision rested upon the abstract interaction of lines and distorted circles, combining free form and rigidity. These were elements that would characterize Art Deco as well. His use of stained glass, muted colors, and wrought iron was widely imitated on the continent, though hardly popular in his own country. In 1904 his Willow Tea Room in Glasgow demonstrated his brilliance; the decoration within the room was an integral part of the whole.

I-1. Arthur Macmurdo's title page for Wren's "City of Churches", 1883, with its swooping, parallel stripes.

I-2. Victor Horta's imaginative, serpentine, ornamental staircase for Tassel House in Brussels, 1892-93.

I-3. The leaded glass doors to the Willow Tea Room in Glasgow, designed by Charles Rennie Macintosh. They combined abstract design of geometric and Art Nouveau elements.

THE VIENNA SECESSION
AND
GUSTAVE KLIMT

In the early years of the century, a group of artists and designers calling itself the Vienna Secession revolted against the official artistic establishment and taste. Josef Hoffmann, a colleague of Mackintosh and one of the two founders, favored a severe and elegant geometry tempered by looping curves and decorative circles in his designs for metalwork and furniture. In 1903 the Weiner Werkstatte began manufacturing objects and furniture designed by members of the Vienna Secession in an attempt to reflect the spirit of their own times. Along with their modernist aims, the Weiner Werkstatte brought new, more contemporary materials into architecture and design, including plate glass, reinforced concrete, linoleum, and aluminum. The Weiner Werkstatte would become an influence on Art Deco in Europe, as well as on the Arts and Crafts Movement in America.

Among the major contributions of Josef Hoffmann was an elaborate home built for Adolphe Stoclet in Brussels. Hoffmann designed everything from grounds and architecture to textiles and furniture; the Palais Stoclet became a showplace for the new modernity. Among the artists who contributed to the décor was Gustave Klimt, the well-known Viennese painter and president of the Vienna Secession. He designed a decorative wall for the Palais Stoclet that combined ornamental curlicues, circles, and squares with symbolist imagery. Working in mosaic, which was to become another hallmark of Art Deco design, he created a series of wall decorations for the Palais Stoclet. With mosaic techniques in marble, glass, and even precious stones, Klimt showed how delicate draftsmanship and abstract illusions—combined with strong spiritual imagery—could mesh in architectural design as well as painting. Following the lead of the Palais Stoclet and other such original buildings, Art Deco would also use the pictorial or abstract mosaic wall to complete the overall decoration of an interior.

I-4. A chair by Josef Hoffmann for the Weiner Werkstatte emphasized repeated parallel loops and new proportions.

I-5. "Fulfillment," c. 1910 was a mosaic of glass, marble, and semi-precious stones, designed by Gustav Klimt and executed by Leopold Forstner for the Palais Stoclet, Brussels.

The stylized "organic naturalism" of Art Nouveau was adapted into Deco design, with patterns that owed much to the earlier style, as well as to the symmetry of Deco. Wrought iron, veneered woods, and fabric were all decorated with patterns reminiscent of the earlier style. The work of two French designers, Maurice Dufrêne and Edgar Brandt, show how the patterns of Art Nouveau influenced Deco design. Dufrene's fabric design, made in the 1920s, and his decorative room design combining curves and angles and repeated organic motifs, were typical of the evolving Parisian style, while Brandt's wrought iron fire screen (c. 1923) adapted the curlicues and contrasting parallel lines that originated in Art Nouveau.

1-7 Edgar Brandt's decorative panel, c. 1923, called "Les Cigones d'Alsace," was made of wrought iron and bronze.

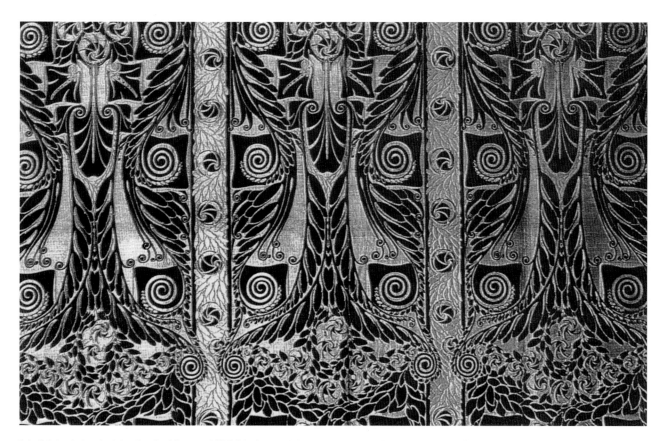

1-6. Fabric design by Maurice Dufrêne, c. 1925-30, featured the "organic naturalism" that would influence Art Deco design.

Carton d'invitation de la Société Maurice Dufrêne.
Ce document à trois volets dont la couverture porte simplement les initiales du décorateur, est une invitation à venir visiter l'exposition consacrée aux œuvres de Maurice Dufrêne, décorateur. L'hôtel était situé au 22 et 22 bis, rue Bayard près des Champs-Elysées. Les amateurs pouvaient y découvrir tout le nécessaire pour embellir leur demeure : "architecture, décors, meubles, tapisserie, peinture, sculpture, papiers peints, tapis, tissus, soieries, broderies, batiks, dentelles, filets, céramiques, vitraux, cristaux, verreries, bijoux, orfèvreries, lustres, appliques, abat-jour, lampes."
Paris, musée des Arts décoratifs.

I-8. An inviation from the Societé Maurice Defrêne pictured a fabric with organic corn shapes, contrasting curving and angular furniture outlines, and overall decorative aesthetic.

I-9. A boudoir designed by Armand-Albert Rateau, 1920-22 for the fashion designer Jeanne Lanvin featured symmetry, deep purple tones, and elegant ornamentation, predating the Deco Exposition.

By the end of the second decade of the twentieth century, curves and swoops of Art Nouveau had become ever more decorative and free-form, with ornamentation throughout the fashionable interior. The stylized leaf and flower motifs, gave a kind of delicately organic view of nature. The three French rooms shown here were designed in the early 1920s; their emphasis on pattern is unmistakable.

I-10. A bedroom designed by Atelier Martine/Paul Biret's Studio School presented low
furniture in front of a glamorously decorated wall.

I-11. A French Deco living room dominated by pattern, both on wall and furniture; as in many such interiors, design focuses on natural images of trees and water.

MODERN PAINTING AND SCULPTURE

The explosion—for that is how it seemed to the previous generation—of modern art in the first two decades of the twentieth century had a profound influence on architecture and the decorative arts. The replacement of recognizable subject matter with "pure" design, the emphasis on planes of space, and the intersection of geometry and the fine arts would all become part of the new Deco trend.

Cubism, Futurism, and Constructivism

Cubism, Futurism and Constructivism—three styles of the new painting- and sculpture-influenced Deco design both artistically and symbolically. Cubism, with its new way of seeing space and objects in geometric terms introduced a fascinating blend of abstract spatial concepts. The sharply defined, three-dimensional lines and intersecting planes of Cubist art trans-

lated effortlessly into the elegant space and complex design of the Deco interior.

Futurism, with its emphasis on conveying a sense of speed and motion, influenced Deco design both with its imagery—repeated arrows and triangles to suggest the thrust of motion, and symbolically, in its quest to show speed and energy. Futurist painting became a prime influence on Deco sculpture and interior decoration.

And in Constructivism, which also sought to suggest the urban, industrial landscape of its time while liberating art from realism, Deco designers found dynamism and exciting divisions of space. Olga Rozanova, a leading Russian painter used the language of abstraction through her brilliant compositions of circles, angles, and dynamic lines. The language of abstraction, with its strong contrast of circles and dynamic lines, contributed to Deco's efforts to convey a sense of the machine age.

I-12. "Landscape" by Juan Gris shows how Cubists saw nature in three-dimensional terms, or planes of space, tipping them slightly to suggest distance; Cubist painting was a major influence on Deco design.

I-13. Olga Rozanova's "Suprematism" of 1916 shows how the leader of the Russian avant-garde wanted to "liberate painting from its subservience to ready-made forms of reality." She used hard-edged abstract forms suggestive of machinery and the urban environment.

I-14. Futurist artist, Umberto Boccioni's print "Those Who Go Away" of 1911 is an example of Futurism's emphasis on motion through dashing parallel lines and repeated angular shapes.

As modern art spread from its birthplace in Paris across Europe and Russia (and eventually to the United States), the influence of painting on commercial design became more and more noticeable. Makers of posters, as well as designers of interiors and furniture, used motion—and particularly speed—as symbols of the new era. New technology also became an inspiration for Deco designers. Following the lead of Futurist painters and sculptors, they tried to create images that reflected the excitement and dynamism of their time. In the 1920s sculptors and poster artists used similar shapes and settings, with elongated, parallel lines, and repeated triangles to suggest flight, airplanes, comets, and high speed, as well as human energy. Dramatic contrasts in dark and light added to these images of energy, which would become central to American Deco too.

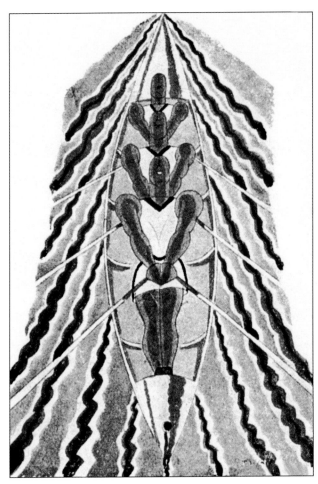

I-16. A 1925 French illustration of rowers uses repeated forms and diagonals to create the illusion of speed and energy.

I-15. Amherst-Villiers poster for airplane races, features elongated triangles and rippling, parallel lines to indicate flight.

Just as the Cubists broke open the cube to assert its three-dimensional essence, the circle was also opened up. The work of both painters and pictorial designers focused on the divided and incomplete circle, and the interior designers soon followed. A typical Deco design employing the broken circle (first explored by painters Robert and Sonia Delaunay) was the 1925 book jacket designed by Pierre Legrain for Alfred deVigny's "Daphne."

A drawing of the same year, by designer Pierre Chareau for a library at the French Embassy in Paris, shows how the circle with a dividing design made its way into the Deco interior, both through architecture and décor. The striking circle in the ceiling of the room is echoed by the round rug, and contrasted dramatically with the vertical columns and horizontal shelving.

I-17. Book binding by Pierre Legrain for "Daphne" by Alfred de Vigny features the open circle and contrasting verticals that would become a popular aspect of Deco design.

I-18. Designer Pierre Chareau's 1925 drawing for the library of a French embassy uses two elements that would typify Art Deco interiors: palmwood paneling and circular design.

I-19. A wall mural painted in France in 1928 creates a dramatic sense of movement and power with its abstract use of repeated stripes and circles.

GEOMETRIC INTERIOR DESIGN:
THE DE STIJL AND
BAUHAUS MOVEMENTS

Architects and interior designers were working with abstract geometric design as early as the first decade of the century. In 1904 the designer Peter Behrens created the interior of a restaurant in Dusseldorf that was a masterpiece of interconnected angles and orderly geometric ornamentation. His use of geometric motifs—from rectangles to squares and diamond shapes—suggest how pervasive was the new interest in modernistic spatial design.

I-20. The elegantly geometric interior of the Jungbrunnen restaurant in Dusseldorf was designed by Peter Behrens in 1904.

By 1917 a group of artists and designers had joined together to reconcile the ideas of modern art with those of design to form the de Stijl ("style") movement in Holland. The de Stijl group, which had tremendous influence, was soon followed by the collective Bauhaus in Germany. These two cooperative movements would become the most important influences on Deco design.

It was the aim of both groups of thinkers and artists to simplify design with interesting architecture and a decorative sense of geometry. De Stijl and then Bauhaus were in themselves strong reactions to the decorative elements of Art Nouveau. Like modernist painting, to which they were so closely allied, the de Stijl movement and then the Bauhaus, rejected the elongated curves and decorative playfulness, as well as the floral imagery, of Art Nouveau.

The de Stijl group was a Dutch cooperative of artists, architects, furniture makers, and designers led by the painters Piet Mondrian and Theo van Doesberg. Their attempt to reconcile Cubist painting with a machine-age aesthetic in both the fine and applied arts led de Stijl toward more and more abstract work. Geometry was a major influence in both their art and interior design, bringing spatial division and angular, intersecting planes of color and line to painting, furniture, architecture, and interior design. A 1924-25 room is a striking example of the use of line and cube, from its geometric lighting fixture to the furniture and carefully placed windows.

Theo van Doesberg, the modernist painter and spokesman for the de Stijl group, presented the interior of a small theater that showed how the geometric forms of painting could be translated into interior design. Designed by artists Jean Arp and Sophie Tauber-Arp, the small café called "l'Aubette" has walls and floors and ceiling decorated in a geometric fashion, accented by colored glass and linear railings.

I-21. The cover of the first issue of the De Stijl magazine, with its architecturally abstract design, was produced by Theo van Doesberg in 1917.

I-22. This functional, abstract, Utrecht interior was a 1924-25 creation of De Stijl designer Gerrit Reitveld.

In 1919 a new institute was founded in Weimar, Germany; the Bauhaus was a larger and more influential, international group of artists and architects, who like their predecessors in the de Stijl movement, wanted to create a functional form of architecture and design. Their aesthetic was clean and pure, taking the form of angular, geometric lines and carefully balanced spaces. Like its spiritual ancestors, Cubist art and the de Stijl designers, Bauhaus came to typify modernity. Bauhaus, which spread the Cubist aesthetic into the decorative arts and architecture, had a strong effect on Art Deco, though it would be mitigated by many opposing influences.

Among the leaders of the Bauhaus was the brilliant painter and theoretician, Wassily Kandinsky. His own living room attests to the power of the Bauhaus aesthetic, with its strong angularity and careful disposition of empty space, as well as its integration of furniture with art and architecture.

1-23. The interior of L'Aubette, a cinema in Strasburg (1927) by Theo van Doesberg, shows how closely interior design paralleled painting in the modernist aesthetic.

I-24. Wassily Kandinsky's dining room (with furniture by Marcel Breuer) where the décor echoes his own paintings on the walls.

I-25. Gunta Stotzl's tapestry for the Bauhaus uses a variety of motifs and patterns that would be translated by generations of designers into both hand-woven and machine-made textiles.

The Bauhaus incorporated all of the aspects of design, from furniture to wall hangings. Even designers of rugs shared the Bauhaus sense of design and integrated décor. Gunta Stotzl, the only woman staff member, was a weaver who translated abstraction into hand-woven, as well as machine-produced, carpets and textiles. Her brilliant weaving included many of the abstract motifs that would be absorbed by Deco designers, from the contrasting curving and angular images, to the wavy parallel lines and squares.

The collaborative nature of the Bauhaus produced extraordinary interaction between the arts. No project was more striking than their Sommerfeld House, a 1921 design featuring woodwork by Josef Schmidt and stained glass by Josef Albers. This geometric façade presaged Deco in many ways, with its stylish use of Cubist design in wood and its overall patterning, as well as its contrasting use of stained glass.

I-26. The 1921 Bauhaus project called Sommerfeld House was a collaborative
effort by Joost Schmidt (woodwork) and Josef Albers (stained glass); it emphasized
geometric design, as well as the importance of craft itself.

Only a short time later, French designers had adopted the Bauhaus vocabulary. Georges Champion, in 1926, and the great designer Jean Dunand, created rooms predicated on the Bauhaus style of geometric balance and unity.

I-27. The smoking room of the French Embassy, suggesting the inside of a cube, was designed by Francis Jourdain, with a black lacquer screen and furniture by Jean Dunand.

I-28. An interior created for Studios Gué, c. 1926, by Georges Champion, was strongly influenced by Bauhaus design.

BALLET AND THEATRICAL DESIGN

The ballets that appeared in Paris, with touring companies from Russia, had a particularly decorative influence on the new design style. Presented with a combination of whimsical modernism and folk images, and featuring brilliant, sometimes lurid, colors and costumes amidst ornate symmetrical arches, curlicues, and turreted castles, these picturesque, playful settings captured the imagination of Parisians. The colors of Russian ballets became fashionable; the pastel tones of Art Nouveau were replaced by "barbaric hues" (as a contemporary critic described them): crimsons and oranges, jade green and deep purple. Ballets by the great choreographers of the early decades of the twentieth century, including Nijinsky and Moiseyev, included figures with stylized gestures and symbolic costumes. These images were picked up by sculptors and became popular in Deco interiors, while the imaginative settings were widely imitated by designers.

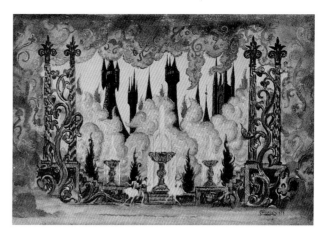

I-29. A setting for the ballet "Raymonda" by Mitislav Dobuzhinsky is an example of the ornamentalism and imagination of Russian theatrical designs that so entranced interior designers.

I-30. A ballet scene from Moiseyev's "The Three Fat Men" with settings by B.A. Matrunin featured the repeated arches that would become characteristic of many Art Deco interiors.

But Russian ballet also brought with it an additional—and very influential—message: the setting for the ballet was an integral part of the action. Deco designers borrowed the idea. Their room designs tried to capture the same fanciful experience, with a variety of patterns, billowing drapery, and tall, decorative walls with arches and built-in paintings. The overall look was akin to a stage setting. In many cases, over-ornamentation won out over the pure rectilinear styles brought about by Bauhaus and other modernist design.

1-31. The Reception Hall from the Paris Exposition in 1925 was designed by André Freschet; it showed some of the influences of ballet settings, including rose tinted drapery and stage-like setting.

The Figure in Motion

The gestures and body positions of the dancers, too, were particularly appealing to Deco designers; human and animal images were "caught" by sculptors in moments of motion or arrested movement, just as though they had been dancing on stage. Sculptor Pierre le Faguays' "Faun and Nymph" was a popular example, while George Valmier's printed harlequin combined Cubist ideas and theatrical gesture.

I-33. George Valmier's Pierrot-like print "Décors et Couleurs" from 1929 shows influences of both theater and modern art.

The beautiful, stylized female figure, often accompanied by a graceful greyhound or a leaping gazelle became popular as well. A ballet called "Les Biches" was said to have influenced a generation of Deco designers with its representation of the leaping gazelle. In fact, numerous Deco items—from sculpture to furniture to glassware—bore the gazelle image along with a profiled figure of a woman, striding or running.

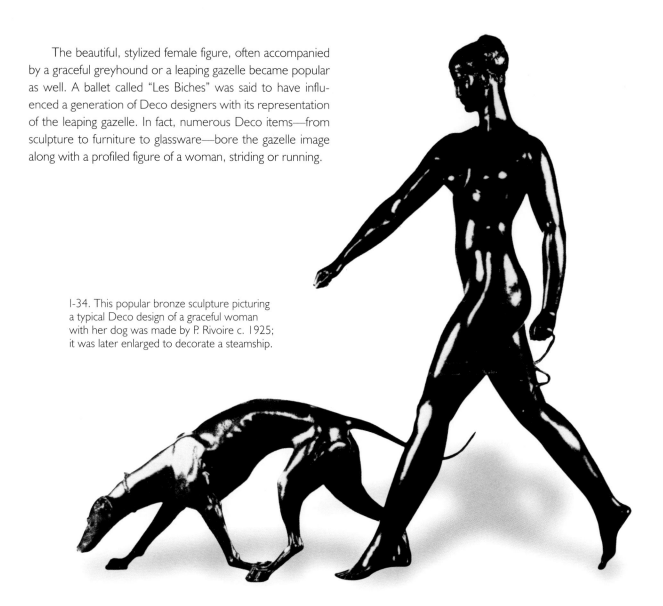

1-34. This popular bronze sculpture picturing a typical Deco design of a graceful woman with her dog was made by P. Rivoire c. 1925; it was later enlarged to decorate a steamship.

The female figure with an animal was meant to suggest both grace and movement that had been suddenly arrested (perhaps with a nod to the new cinematic techniques). The bronze sculpture shown here was part of a group by French artist P. Rivoire; it was made around 1925, and was later enlarged to decorate the steamship "L'Atlantique."

Three images celebrating the opening of the 1925 Paris Exposition bear the similarly graceful, stylized figures surrounded by plant designs that came to characterize so much Art Deco design. The announcement for the original Exposition Internationale des Arts Decoratifs et Industriels Modernes—from which Art Deco got its name—bore a gracefully dancing female figure with a leaping gazelle, while a celebratory medal showed a typically draped, curving, female figure. And the 1925 cover of the magazine, "L'Illustration," features a combination of many of these decorative influences into one whole. Celebrating the Exposition in Paris, this design included many of the elements that we have come to identify as Deco: the wavy lines, circles, and arches of nature and machine, the formally posed symbolic women with dog and faun, the geometric boundaries and stylized leaves, and the zigzags amid intersecting patterns.

I-35. The official poster for the Paris Exposition of 1925 was designed by Robert Bonfils, with characteristic moving figure, fawn, and plants.

I-36. A bronze medal from the Paris Exposition bears a typically draped, curving female image surrounded by flowers.

I-37. The cover of "l'Illustration" was devoted to the Paris Exposition; it includes many of the motifs and design elements that came to characterize the Art Deco style.

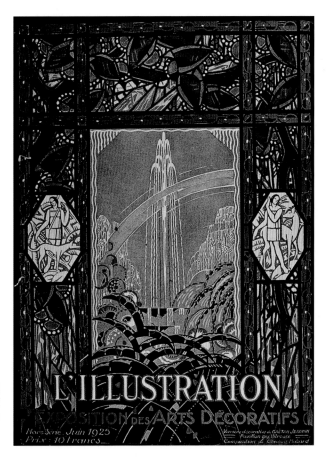

Exotic Sources

Russian ballet sets were not the only exotic source for Deco inspiration. As designers looked for new aesthetic influences, a great variety of odd and exotic sources became popular. Though ancient Egyptian or American Indian symbols, for example, had vogues in various periods, no one era absorbed so many exotic design elements at the same time as Art Deco.

But a confluence of events and discoveries, as well as a new freedom to pursue the outlandish and original, brought Art Deco's creators a vast field of influences to play with. Mixing and matching elements as disparate as the designs of Russian ballet sets and costumes, Mayan temples, and Egyptian tomb art led to many elements of the wildly fanciful Deco style.

Native American Art and Architecture

Native American art and architectural forms were new and stimulating to Europeans. Thus, the great temples of Central America, with their step-like silhouettes brought the pyramid shape and stepped profile to staircases and furniture, lamps and radios. The pyramid became an important Deco design element, appearing again and again in the interior (as well as in the exterior shape of many buildings, particularly in America).

The geometric swirls and interlocking cubes of American Indian pottery, such as that from the Southwest Acoma Indians, and the stripes and zigzags of Navajo rugs fascinated French designers. They imitated the parallel stripes and intersecting circles, and even produced the deep earth tones characteristic of Native American arts. In some examples Mexican cactus shapes replaced the fern motif that had been so popular in previous design.

I-38. The pyramid temple, "El Castillo" at Chichen Itza in Mexico has the distinctive stepped sides that became popular in Deco furniture and wall design.

I-39. Southwest Native American pottery motif, such as this Acoma example, captured the attention of European designers.

I-40. Navajo blanket features stripes, parallel ripple lines, and deep warm colors.

I-41. The main entrance to the International Theater Exposition in Amsterdam bears exotic designs derived from other cultures on its wall panels and columns.

The use of these primitive designs, combined with the newest in Bauhaus angularity can be seen in a curious entrance to a theatre in Amsterdam that predated the Art Deco exhibition in Paris by several years. Large columns decorated with curves and curlicues reminiscent of American Indian pottery contrast with the formal planes dividing the space.

Ancient Egyptian Art and Architecture

Ancient Egyptian art was another source that captured the imagination of Deco designers. Long popular, particularly in early nineteenth century England and France, Egyptian tomb art had a new vogue after the discovery of King Tutankhamon's tomb in 1922. Both the intricate patterning of the jewelry and the serene wall reliefs in profile became sources of exotic design. The smooth-sided pyramid shape, the sleek golden figures of gods and goddesses, and the surrounding stripes, small circles, and stylized hieroglyphics of Egyptian art were imitated in mosaic work, jewelry, and sculpture in the Deco era. Many large reliefs portraying symbolic figures decorated both interior and exterior walls. Doorways, in particular, borrowed from the Egyptian, both in shape and motif: there were scarabs and Egyptian cats, Cleopatra-like heads, sphinx, stylized palms, and complicated mosaic patterns of gems and enamel-work.

I-42. Egyptian winged goddess Mut appears on an ancient bracelet of gold and glass; Egyptian images and hieroglyphics became widely popular in Europe after Tutankhamon's tomb was discovered.

I-43. A French Art Deco bracelet of diamonds, rubies, and sapphires is decorated with Egyptian-style animal-headed bed, small decorative motifs and hieroglyphics.

Asian Arts

Asian art was another exotic influence. Japanese woodblocks, already made popular in late nineteenth century France (and so influential to Impressionist painting) brought a dramatic combination of contrasting straight and curving lines, directional changes, and bold color. And Chinese tile design used symbolic parallel waves that became a standard of Deco imagery.

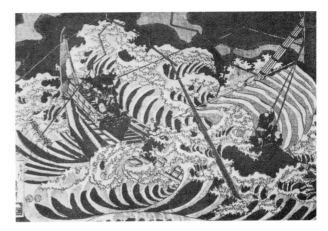

I-44. A Japanese woodblock print from Edo-era Japan uses repeated stripes and wave motif to create a sense of movement.

I-45. A Ming Dynasty Chinese tile design employs the decorative overlapping wave motif that would appear time and again in Deco design.

It is not hard to find Deco examples that were influenced by Asian design; many of these influences can be seen in typical sculptures of the Deco era, and in other decorative objects. Maurice Guiraud-Riviere's "The Comet," which was a bronze allegory suggesting a woman's figure as a speeding comet is one example. Its emphasis on speed and dynamism is typically Art Deco, and its design reminds us both of the emphasis on motion in Futurist art, and Chinese wave motifs. The Japanese fan dancer is even more obviously Asian in concept; the figure was made in Germany in 1929.

I-46. Maurice Guirard-Rivière's gilt and bronze sculpture on a marble base was called "The Comet;" it combines Chinese wave motif with Deco emphasis on speed.

I-47. A popular fan statuette, made in Germany in 1929, is even more directly influenced by Asian art.

I-48. A Jean Dunand study for a gold and black lacquer panel (designed for a steamship) uses Asian wave and bird motifs in contrasting directions to create a typically Deco sense of motion and elegance.

Jean Dunand, the great French Deco designer, created one of the best known pieces of his era: a panel made of gold and black lacquer, designed for the ocean liner Atlantique. In its elegant design, symbolic cranes reminiscent of Japanese prints nestle among parallel rippling and straight lines, whose directions also suggest the spatial designs of early modern art.

GLASS DESIGN AND ELECTRICITY

Another major source of Deco was the new work of glass designers. Due to them, light—both natural and artificial—became an increasingly important element of the Art Deco interior. While glass windows and doors had long been ornamental, and were a major element of design in Charles Rennie Mackintosh's interiors and Tiffany's designs, for example, the use of entire walls of etched or illuminated glass panels became a popular Deco element. Not coincidentally, brilliant glassmakers like René Lalique, whose freestanding glass objects, like the panel of nudes and curlicues seen here, expanded the vocabulary of technique and style in glasswork.

Complete walls of glass executed by Lalique graced several rooms at the Paris Exposition of 1925. Two examples were typically Deco in their design of nature's burgeoning forms. In one, a dining room featured glass walls designed by a painter named Raymond Quibel. In another Lalique setting, an incised glass forest of graceful trees with a boar hunt, done in silver on glass, created an entirely new sense of interior light.

I-49. Glass doors by René Lalique were made for a train; Lalique's designs used glass in a new way, with graceful line and repeated motifs.

I-50. The dining room at the Paris Exposition had an extraordinary glass wall designed by Raymond Quibel and executed by René Lalique.

I-51. The marble walls of Lalique-designed dining room at the Exposition were incised and silvered with a forest scene and a wild boar hunt, to contrast with the modernist grid on floor and ceiling.

But it was the influence of electricity that had the strongest impact on glass design, for electric lighting behind glass became a popular component of the Deco interior. With the advent of widespread artificial light, interior design embraced electricity as a major part of room décor—particularly in public spaces.

This 1907 lithograph by designer Peter Behrens gives an early clue to how electricity was viewed in almost romantic terms, with thousands of small starry dots suggesting its broad reach. In a strikingly contemporary look even today, Deco designers began using electricity to illuminate entire panels and to accent architecture in a new and striking way. Typical were the Grand Hotel in Dax, which included a brilliant geometric glass tile installation, and the foyer of the Strand Palace Hotel in London, where architectural outlines were accented by lighted glass.

I-52. Peter Behren's poster for AEG from 1907; electricity is already seen as an exciting decorative element.

I-53. Lighted glass panels in the halls of the Grand Hotel in Dax, France, featured individual glass tiles engraved and encrusted with bits of pressed glass.

I-54. The foyer of the Strand Palace Hotel in London was designed by Oliver P. Bernard. It featured a brand new combination of geometric design and electricity. (Dismantled as "tacky" in 1960, it was saved, reconstructed, and exhibited recently at the Victoria and Albert Museum.)

THE STYLE OF THE FUTURE

Closely related to the emphasis on electric light was the burgeoning interest in machinery itself. Deco arrived just as industrialism and machinery had changed European life forever. The machine aesthetic had already become an important element in modern art, with leading figures like painter Fernand Leger using machine imagery in his painting. Modernist artist and architect, le Corbusier not only described the house as "a machine for living," but also saw mass-production and technology as integral parts of a new utopia.

Art Deco would become the first design style to embrace mass production. And machine imagery would also take its place in the design of the time. (Although it was American Art Deco that fully integrated the machine aesthetic into the Deco interior.) And the materials of industry, that had hitherto been uncommon in interior design and furniture—such as tubular steel and nickel silver, would add to the modern look of Deco design.

Thus, though the Deco mode popularized in France sprang from a variety of historical sources, it effectively supplanted traditional historic architecture—at this time the Beaux Arts style. By turning away from the immediate past, the eclectic, chic Deco style embraced the new and modern, and was immediately seen as a style of the future.

FURNITURE DESIGN

Just as the Deco interior incorporated a great variety of materials and motifs, with patterns and imagery throughout, Deco furniture used similarly disparate elements. Drawing on both the geometric proportions of modernism and the exoticism of foreign and ancient styles, Deco furniture was distinctive—different looking—from that which had come before it. It seemed modern and stylish, and it was soon in great demand.

The Deco furniture designer saw himself as an artist-decorator, whose contributions were part of an integrated composition of architecture, textiles, art, wallpaper, lighting—and furniture. Using the finest woods, elegant finishes, marble tops, inlays, and contrasting rare woods, these carefully calibrated designs were opulent and elegant.

With its combination of many woods and veneers, inlays, glass, metal work, and original design, Deco furniture became a central and eye-catching element of the Deco interior, often repeating elements of design on the walls, or contrasting with them. In the examples seen here, the emphasis on style, dramatic shape, elongated lines, and pattern are all evident, for French Deco furniture was in effect a miniature version of the interior design itself. Chief among these furniture makers were the Dominique firm and Jules Leleu, whose work can be seen among the examples that follow.

I-55. French designer Jules Leleu's Deco furniture, included this freestanding amboyna root mirror in a marble, paneled setting.

I-56. The furniture in Dominique's office setting replicates the angles and woods of surrounding décor.

I-57. A bedroom on a barge from the Paris Exposition in 1925 has contrasting patterns throughout.

Examples by Maurice Dufrêne, Jules Leleu, Dominique, Albert Cheuret, and others, of French Deco furniture featuring geometric design, complex combinations of materials, inlays, and fine fabrics.

I-58. Maurice Dufrêne's commode of rosewood, oak, darker woods, and mother of pearl inlay, c. 1922.

I-59. Amboyna vanity with mirror and ivory detailing by Leleu.

I-60. 1928 secretary by designer Dominique; it is made of rosewood and parchment.

I-61. Armchair by Dominique with ebony and metal filaments.

I-62. Lyre-shaped glass-topped table is by Dominique, c. 1932.

I-63. Leleu's sideboard has mirror and objets d'art; designed for Paris Exposition, it is made of fine amboyna inlaid with ivory.

I-64. Armchair by Leleu has wood feet, chrome accents, and typically Deco proportions.

I-65. Dominique created this side chair
made of wood with gilt circa 1924.

I-66. Leleu Modernist mirrored round table was made c. 1936.

I-67. Sideboard with chandelier and patterned hanging

I-68. A 1930s armoire with ivory and sharkskin inlays.

I-69. Bed, designed by Dominique, dates to around 1928.

I-70. Gilt and wood mantel clock, circa 1920.

I-71. Silvered bronze and alabaster
lamp by Albert Cheuret, c. 1925

I-72. Lamp with globe held by white metal figure with
green-bronze finish was made c. 1928 by Max le Verrier.

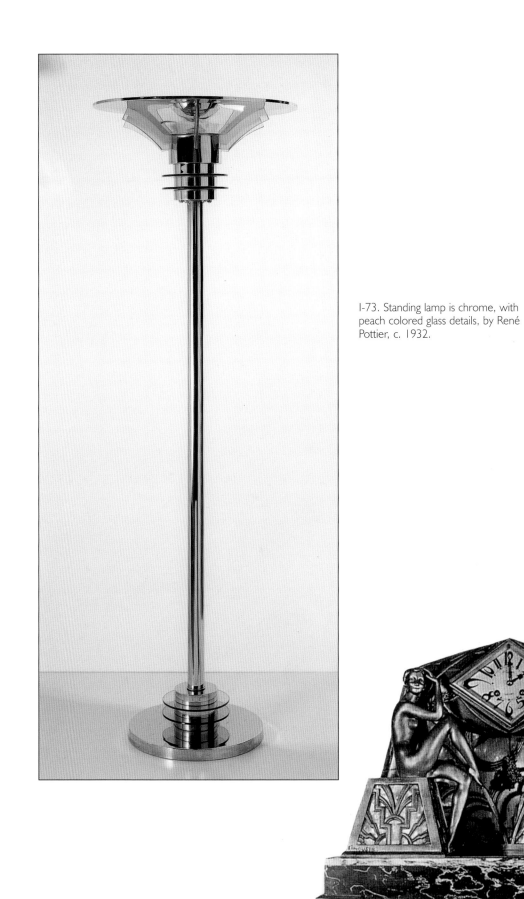

I-73. Standing lamp is chrome, with peach colored glass details, by René Pottier, c. 1932.

I-74. Metal mantel clock on marble base is signed Limousin, 1925.

PART II

THE ORIGINS OF
AMERICAN ART DECO

Before the 1925 Deco exhibition in Paris, the United States had little by the way of a design movement itself. Though a growing source for European designers, with its exciting mix of the new, the technological, the jazzy, and the optimistic, Deco did not take root in Americas as a full-fledged design phenomenon when it did in Europe. While Europeans saw America as a cradle of the New Age that Deco designers sought to reflect, Americans were more conservative.

In the United States a vast mix of different design elements was influenced by geography, various cultural groupings, and primarily a taste for historical styles. Thus the first decades of the twentieth century saw conservative design modes and taste in art and architecture throughout the nation. Many artists and designers with avant-garde ideas gave up hope of bridging the cultural gap between European and American style, and moved to Paris or other European capitals.

HOMEGROWN INFLUENCES

Nonetheless, there were distinct American elements that would influence what would become the Deco movement in this country. First, and perhaps most important, was the skyscraper, an American invention. It had already become the symbol of a city's greatness and style long before the Deco movement. As the skyscraper came to represent the stylish modernity of American cities, urban architecture in New York, Chicago, and other major centers turned increasingly to higher and higher buildings that combined their tall straight verticality with ornament, and with elaborate interiors.

In New York, as early as 1913, Cass Gilbert designed the Woolworth Building, with its contrasting vertical lines and horizontal accents, paving the way for Deco skyscrapers. Well before the Deco movement the skyscraper in New York had evolved into a ziggurat-shaped building, with its characteristic stepped profile. There were two reasons for this design's popularity; one was the influence of Pre-Columbian and ancient Near Eastern pyramid shapes. But just as important, was the zoning requirement in 1916 by the city of New York that required tall buildings to taper toward the top, thus allowing light and air to their neighbors. Before long, the ziggurat shape became popular not only for buildings, but for radios, jewelry, and furniture.

American Skyscrapers

Among the most important homegrown influences on Deco design were the contributions of several leading designers in America: the furniture designer, Gustav Stickley, the glass designer, Louis Comfort Tiffany, and the great architect Frank Lloyd Wright. These three men, whose work predated the Deco era by decades, initiated modernism in the United States.

The Arts and Crafts Movement, under the direction of Stickley created simple, geometric furniture that was influential in turning American design away from the fussiness of the Victorian interior. Although the Arts and Crafts aesthetic insisted on the hand made (and Deco would embrace the machine made), nevertheless the clean lines and geometric proportions of Stickley's designs had a definite impact on the Deco style.

Louis Comfort Tiffany expanded the vocabulary of glass making in both window design and objets d'art. His beautifully colored and gracefully designed glasswork presaged the emphasis on glass in Deco design. His introduction of native-American motifs and a high degree of sophistication in both style and content led to countless Deco details in glass—both from his own workshop and others.

II-1. The 1913 Woolworth Building in New York, designed by Cass Gilbert, was a precursor of Art Deco architecture.

II-2. By the time the step-shaped Paramount Building in New York (designed by C.W. and George L. Rapp) was completed in 1926, it featured such Deco elements as an ornate clock tower with an illuminated glass ball at the top.

II-3. Gustav Stickley emphasized the use of wood and geometric design, as well as a handmade, rough-hewn look.

II-4. A Favrile glass vase by Louis Comfort Tiffany shows the elegance of line, deep color, and fine workmanship that strongly influenced Deco glassmakers.

Frank Lloyd Wright

But it was Frank Lloyd Wright who had the most profound effect on homegrown American design, and subsequently on Art Deco. Early in the century he abandoned the American Victorian for a new and stunning geometric formalism. His sleek lines and ornamental leaded glass designs showed many of the same characteristics as those acclaimed by the Deco movement decades later. It was Wright who exaggerated long lines—in the vertical and horizontal dimensions of a room, and who combined the geometric elements of circle and rectangle to create abstract form.

Wright's innovations in architectural, glass, and furniture design pioneered the use of abstraction in the interior. Though his work grew out of the Arts and Crafts Movement, in which the handmade was prized, Wright also predated the Deco era by approving machine production of furniture, and by making use of Mayan and other exotic design details. He was one of the first designers to integrate electric light into the house interior, and indeed to unify all of the elements of the interior design.

In Wright's Unity Temple of 1906 (built some twenty years before the Deco style took hold), the geometric design is reminiscent of Vienna, as well as of Cubist art, with its emphasis on intersecting rectangular form. And typical of his early stained glass is the window for the Dana Thomas House; its geometric complexity typified his expansion of design into every element of the interior.

II-5. Frank Lloyd Wright's Unity Temple of 1906 clearly demonstrated the architect's interest in geometric formalism and the use of wood. Both elements would become hallmarks of American Deco.

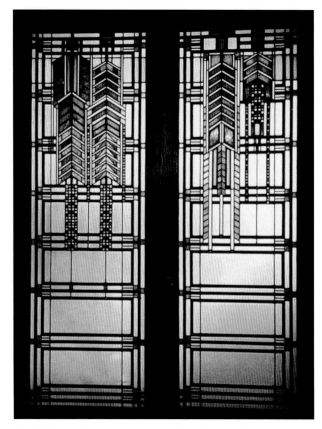

11-6. Stained glass windows in the Dana-Thomas House were designed by Frank Lloyd Wright in 1903; Wright used brilliant color and carefully arranged combinations of geometric forms, as would later Deco designers.

As in Europe, the fine arts of painting and sculpture played a part in bringing about Deco design in the United States. As in Europe, Cubism and other early forms of modernism, emphasizing the geometric, influenced interior design. The first American modernist painters (mostly trained abroad) brought a new sense of the abstract power of curve and cube to the United States. Stanton Macdonald-Wright and Victor Harles were two American pioneer modernists who explored the abstract relationships of form and color. The circles and strong rectangular forms of machinery were reflected in American avant-garde art in the first two decades of the 20th century, though only a very small segment of the American public tolerated any form of abstraction.

American Modern Art

Sculptor John Storrs's abstract works of this early period would come to typify the Deco thrust of verticality and spatial unity; in fact, some of his sculptures seemed to be the prototypes of the modernist architecture that followed. Alexander Archipenko, an émigré to America, brought his sleek, steel figures to this country, where they helped influence the Deco aesthetic; both their shiny, reflective surface and elongated lines predated the Deco era. American Gaston Lachaise's graceful, curving forms with their original, but symmetrically balanced unity (as in his "Peacocks" of 1918 and "Dolphin Fountain" of 1924) influenced Deco imagery. These artists and others would, in fact, help sculpture to become an integral part of the Deco interior.

11-7. American painter Stanton Macdonald-Wright was an early abstractionist who worked with pulsating colors and circular forms, as in "Synchromie in Red," of 1914.

II-8. "Cubist Portrait" by American Victor Harles was painted c. 1920. Cubist interest in spatial planes and interlocking geometric unity influenced early Deco designers in the U.S. as well as Europe.

THE EUROPEAN STYLE ARRIVES

The arrival of many European artists and designers in America had a major impact on the cultural scene and the development of Deco (as well as the other arts) in the 1920s, particularly in New York From theatrical designers to weavers, architects and furniture makers, hundreds of talented people steeped in the European styles of modernism came to make a new creative life in America. It was their input that helped bring about the merging of the European and American Deco aesthetic.

Like their European counterparts, American artists and designers discovered the exotic. References to ancient Egyptian, Pre-Columbian, and other cultures appeared in design in the early decades of the century. And the Harlem Renaissance in the early 1920s also contributed a thoroughly American idiom, not only with the widespread appreciation of jazz (which was picked up in Europe too), but in its stylized images of masks and carvings with African roots.

Many such references appeared in newly designed, fashionable nightspots and public lobbies. The small but stunning lobby at the Film Center in New York suggests how exotic Aztec design influenced the design.

11-10. "Flat Torso" was a work by Alexander Archipenko that introduced the use of long, sleek, semi-abstract figures and shiny metals.

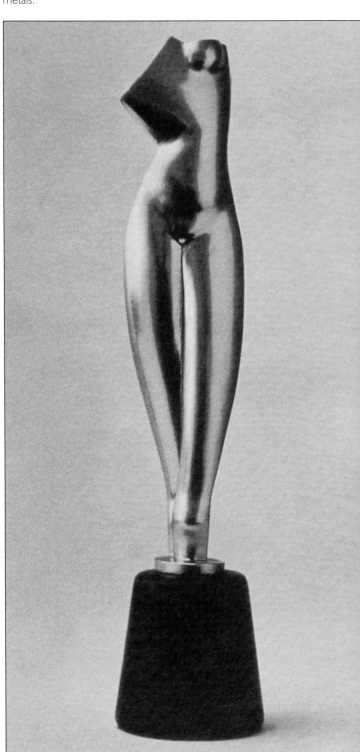

11-9. "Forms in Space" (c. 1926) by John Storrs was typical of his abstract sculptures suggesting the urban landscape's verticality and thrust.

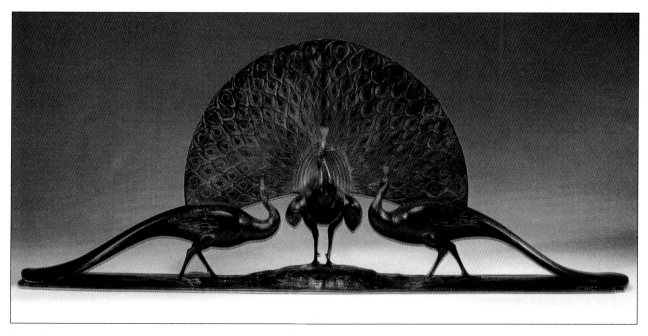

II-11. "The Peacocks" c. 1918 was one of many works by Gaston Lachaise with the long curving lines, symmetry, and burnished metal surfaces that were imitated by Deco designers.

II-12. "Dolphin Fountain of 1924 was another Lachaise work that emphasized interlocking curves and movement, as well as the natural subject matter that appealed to the Deco taste.

11-13. The small, but spectacular lobby of New York's Film Center Building, designed by Jacques Ely Kahn, featured a brilliant mixture of gold, marble, speed stripes, and—like many Deco buildings—Aztec or other Native American design.

THE MACHINE AGE

Perhaps the most important influence of all was the Machine Age itself. As electricity and modern machinery revolutionized American life and its landscape, art and design borrowed heavily from the streamlined look and materials of factories and transportation. From trains to smokestacks, electric advertisements to the wheels of industry, new design reflected an upbeat, exciting future.

It would be the American emphasis on progress and the sleek effects of aerodynamic and industrial imagery that would turn European Deco into the American streamlined style. The chic look of American machine-inspired design would merge with European Deco's deep tones, reflective surfaces, and elegant proportions. Long before the 1925 Exposition in Paris, American artists and designers were experimenting with the new idioms of modern art and industry. In 1915 the San Francisco Exposition featured a "Fountain of Energy" by Alexander Stirling Calder; its theme was progress and science.

Thus, by 1925 when the Paris Expo formally introduced the Deco idiom to the world, the United States was already experimenting with "modernism" of its own, relating home-grown design to the cosmopolitan images from abroad.

Though the United States did not take part in the Expo itself, more than 100 American designers and representatives of industry and design institutions attended and reported home. Soon a show of designs from the Expo began touring American cities. The international acclaim that the Expo occasioned put an official seal of approval on the new style. And it was not until Deco had been transformed into a more American style that it truly caught on in the nation.

From then on various cities in the United States strove mightily to appear stylish and up-to-date. New York and cities across the country produced major buildings that were elaborately designed and decorated within. In New York, dozens of new skyscrapers were built in the Deco style (many can still be visited). The brilliant Chrysler Building, with its machine imagery, and the Empire State Building, with its tall mast designed as a mooring for dirigibles, were only two of the numerous landmark Deco buildings. Among the many others were the Barclay-Vesey Building, the Twentieth Century Fox Building, the complex at Rockefeller Center, and the Film Center Building, one of some thirty Deco buildings designed by noted architect Jacques Ely Kahn.

AN ARCHITECTURAL
EXPLOSION

Throughout the nation major Deco sites appeared; among the most notable were Union Terminal in Cincinnati, the Circle Tower Building in Indianapolis, Syracuse's Niagara Mohawk Building, Detroit's Union Trust Building, and Kansas City's Municipal Auditorium and K.C. Power and Light Building. All across the country cities took pride in constructing Deco-style buildings; there were major outposts in Chicago, Houston, Atlanta, Cleveland, Omaha, and Kalamazoo, among others.

In California numerous buildings—ranging from a Los Angeles department store to theaters across the state from Oakland to Catalina Island—were created with Deco interiors that featured elaborate murals, furniture, and lighting. Aztec designs were popular, as were all kinds of exotic detailing. Indeed, the burgeoning movie industry's "picture palaces" became fanciful centers of design. Examples of Deco architecture (and excess) could be found in theaters all over the country, including the Paramount in Oakland, the Wiltern in Los Angeles, the Roxy in New York, the Colony in Cleveland, and the Paramount in Aurora, Illinois.

II-14 to 11-16. The Chrysler Building designed by William Van Alen and completed in 1930 displayed automobile imagery both in its tower design and in masonry car images horizontally ornamenting the building. The lobby of the Chrysler Building was characterized by fine woods, opulent onyx, and gleaming surfaces in geometric design.

The Chrysler Building

II-14

II-15

II-16

II-17. An example of a 1939 Deco picture palace was the Roxy Theater at Radio City, New York, with its heady mix of exotic detail and ornamentation.

Miami Deco

In Miami, an entire area became an Art Deco resort. The development of the waterfront coincided with the height of Deco stylishness in the 1930s. Tropical Deco had its own particular flavor: there were balconies, cantilevered sunshades over windows, sea motifs and sunrises imbedded in the Deco imagery, porthole windows, curved outlines, and a general taste for glamour and brilliant, deep color.

II-18. The Marlin Hotel, built in 1939, was renovated fifty years later; its distinctive curved lines and outlining in blue neon make it a focus of the Deco resort area.

What gave these interiors their Deco look? The rhythms of the Jazz Age, the fantasies of the movie culture, the popularity of fast cars and travel, and a native optimism—these were characteristics of American life that combined with the sophisticated European style to create American Deco. Some Deco design came directly from Europe: a graceful French import for the new Rockefeller Center shows one way the Deco style took its place in the United States. A sculptural panel called "Beaute" by the noted French sculptor Alfred Auguste Janniot was brought to New York for the "French Building" of the complex. Made in 1932, it brought a European taste of elegance, symbolism, and glamour. But most of what we today know as Art Deco in America was homegrown.

In fact, American Deco was so varied a style that the most elaborate and the most austere both merited the name. Three distinct design elements, however, can be identified: zigzag moderne, featuring geometric and stylized motifs drawn from ancient art and nature's forms; streamlined, which bore a futuristic, aerodynamic look; and neo-classical, which was influenced by a simplified, symmetrical stylization. A pictorial tour and analysis of the American Deco idiom shows the variety and glamour of the style, and why it is now being revived.

II-19. "Beauté," a rare plaster sculpture by Alfred Auguste Janniot, made in France for the "French Building" at Rockefeller Center, c. 1932; it typifies Deco emphasis on the symbolic, with mythic female form, growing plants, and graceful line.

PART III

THE DECO INTERIOR

American Art Deco flourished all across the nation in the late 1920s and 1930s. It was a popular movement both with the public, and with its creators—the artists, architects, crafts makers, and furniture designers who gave the style its American version. For as a design style, "Deco" was an umbrella term that gave unusual freedom to these creative people, providing them with opportunities to produce their own imaginative versions of a highly popular style, while still working within a particular framework. The artists and architects became both tastemakers and purveyors of a national design idiom.

American Deco was both a national style, appealing to the country's taste and mood, and a regional one, incorporating vernacular and regional motifs. Thus, American exuberance and energy were symbolized, as well as all kinds of regional motifs. It was this heady combination of idioms and symbols within brilliant architectural frameworks that came to be known as Art Deco in this country.

Although the American version of the style incorporated so many historical, and exotic, and contemporary ideas and influences, it nonetheless had certain uniform characteristics that made it identifiably Art Deco. The following pages present a sampling of stylistic traits.

SPATIAL HARMONY AND ORNAMENTATION

Art Deco emphasized design; its interiors were carefully organized with a sense of spatial harmony. Like the abstract painting of its time, geometry was a major influence; straight lines and curves were contrasted in both large and small ways. Tall verticals were balanced by ornamental strips and curves, graceful proportion was a major consideration, and the overall ambiance—from materials to decoration—was designed with an eye to balance that was almost classical in its symmetry and weight.

The geometric elements were notable in both the overall layout of rooms and in the architectural details. Early in the Deco era the vertical was stressed; by the mid-30s there was a more horizontal emphasis as "streamline modernism" became popular. But in both periods, the same stress on balance and contrasting lines and curves was evident.

Interactive curves and straight lines appeared in numerous ways: in the lobby of the Kansas City Municipal Building we see the long straight verticals contrasting with circular elements on floor, wall, and ceiling. In a dining room from Cranbrook, where the great Finnish designer Eero Saarinen explored modernistic design, a great circular light in the ceiling is contrasted with geometric forms throughout the harmonious room. In fact, the overall proportional harmony in the Deco room created a receptive space for a highly ornamental style of design.

III-1. The dining room at Saarinen House (1928-30) in Cranbrook, Michigan, had a circular ceiling light, which was echoed by the round table, and contrasted with the patterned rug, step-shaped cabinet design, and vertical accents throughout the room.

III-2. The mezzanine lobby of the Kansas City Municipal Auditorium was decorated with circular motifs on ceiling and floor, in addition to murals by Walter Alexander Bailey, and strong vertical accents throughout the room.

THE MOTIFS

American Art Deco was characterized by a variety of surface and sculptural decoration. One of the most ornamental styles in history, American Deco reveled in design—from the shape of a cigarette case to the grand sculptural panels on a skyscraper. The use of motif as an integral part of the overall design was central to Art Deco's appeal. In addition to abstract motifs, pictorial images carried all kinds of symbolic messages for the new modern age, and the motifs themselves echoed and played off the architecture surrounding them. This fashionable use of elaborate ornamentation gave artists and architects the opportunity to use a variety of motifs and patterns, many of which were drawn from exotic and historical sources, aesthetic movements of the past, and new images of the Machine Age, as well as abstract geometry.

Geometric

In fact, we see the same elements of geometry in the smallest motifs as well as well as in larger architectural proportions. The contrast of straight and circular was continued in the small designs and furniture of the Deco interior. The interactive curves and straight lines appear on the sculptured facades of building walls and in the extravagant mo-

saics and metalwork adorning interiors of new buildings of the time. The more elaborate of these designs resembled kaleidoscope images with their symmetrical intricacy. Fan shapes, ziggurats, and chevrons were among the most popular symmetrical motifs.

III-3. The Wiltern Theater in Los Angeles presented a typically decorative wall motif of zigzag and circles.

III-4. This example of a geometric grillwork design is from the Governor Hotel in Miami.

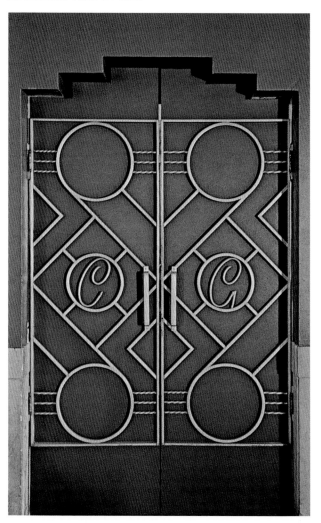

III-5. A section of the colorful mosaic, with a geometric design resembling a view through a kaleidoscope, appears in the lobby of an Ely Jacques Kahn building at 2 Park Avenue in New York.

Abstract Design

But rigid geometric designs of squares, circles, and triangles were not the only type of abstract element. Free-form abstract designs were also characteristic of this mix, with interlocking triangles, segmented circles, exuberant spirals, swoops, parallel wavy lines, ziggurat shapes, and zigzags. As great swoops reminiscent of Art Nouveau and zigzagging diagonals upset the orderly geometry of verticals and perfect circles, the Art Deco idiom achieved an increasingly free-spirited aura. Particularly exuberant were the designs for movie theaters and public lobbies, but these design elements reached the smallest venues as well. It was this free use of abstract elements that gave the Deco interior a playful charm and grace that contrasted effectively with the severity of the architectural proportions.

III-6. A screen from the Chanin Building in New York shows the ornamental use of bronze; it is just one of many Deco adornments in this exuberant building.

III-7. Brass radiator grills in the lobby of 420 Madison Avenue in New York have a brilliantly free design of spirals, loops, and directional thrusts.

Nature

In addition to these abstract motifs, Art Deco turned to more symbolic images in the grillwork, carvings, and other decorations that adorned their buildings. Chief among these motifs were designs borrowed from nature, including plants, animals, the solar system, lightning, and rushing water. The wealth of natural imagery emphasized growing, burgeoning plants, and expressions of nature's energy.

The most common motifs included growing flowers, unfurling plant fronds, and decorative leaves. In repetitive, intricate, and stylized designs suggesting profuse gardens and forests, Deco plant designs covered screens, radiators, doors, and anywhere ornamental metalwork or wall design could be implemented.

III-9. A plaster ornamental panel from the Wiltern Theater has a motif of unfurling plant fronds as its theme.

III-10. Leaf pattern from a wall fabric at the old Suffolk Theater on Long Island is typical of Deco plant imagery.

III-8. The repeated motif in the entrance decoration of the Cheney Building in New York suggests a field of growing plants.

III-11. Grillwork of stylized flowers appears over the lobby cigar
stand at 60 Wall Tower in New York.

Natural and Man-made Energy

No motifs were more indicative of the era than were expressions of energy, both natural and man-made. Natural energy, as suggested by stylized zig-zags of lightning and thunderbolts, and brilliant sun-bursts were typical design motifs. Astrological imagery and personifications of these forces of nature were seen in murals, metalwork, and sculpture. Ornamental grillwork, used for elevator gates and windows were adorned with lightning bolts, while ceilings and walls were decorated with bursting suns and their decorative rays.

III-12. Radiator grill from the Chanin Building has cosmic imagery; its free-form, abstract lines suggest nature's power as it surrounds the city.

III-13. The bronze bas relief from the old Daily News Building is typical of a Deco stylized landscape of sunrise.

III-14. "Achievement," a sculpted relief by René Chambellan from the Chanin Building, bears Deco sun imagery and man's harnessing of its power. It is one of several plaster reliefs painted with bronze patina.

III-15. A much more elaborate sunburst is the central decoration of the ceiling of the Deco landmark Barclay Vesey Building in New York.

III-16. The extraordinary sunburst from the ceiling of the Wiltern Theater creates a strong illusion of the sun's rays and powers.

Fountains and Rushing Water

Fountains and rushing water similarly symbolized the forces of nature, rendered in regular, symmetrical forms. Water being poured or elegantly rising from a fountain suggested both nature's beauty and man's control, for the natural forces portrayed by Deco designers were never wild or out of control, a point emphasized by the careful symmetry of each design.

III-17. A typically symmetrical and controlled fountain decorated a theater lobby wall; the image, just above the stepped wood molding, was repeated at intervals throughout the interior.

III-18. A model of the "Oasis" screen by the noted Deco designer, Edgar Brandt, shows a fountain set amidst a sea of stylized flowers and leaves.

III-19. A Deco wall relief from the Mellon Bank in Los Angeles features, like many motifs of the time, a stylized figure working in tandem with nature—in this case, pouring water from an urn and activating a water wheel.

III-21. Two swans amid ornamental flowers decorate a wall in the Deco-style Netherlands Plaza Hotel in Cincinnati.

Stylized, Symmetrical Animals and Birds

Stylized animals and birds were among the most common motifs. Greyhounds, fauns, happily leaping gazelles, and swans, usually seen against a background of stylized plants and flowers and curlicues were widely pictured. Such designs were often framed by octagonal, pyramid-shaped, or other geometric borders. Within the confining shape portrayals of animals and birds were cheerful, benign, and symmetrical. Nature in these pictorial decorations was always controlled and ornamental.

III-22. A stylized deer against a leafy octagonal pattern is typical of Deco era animal and plant motifs. It appears as a wall decoration in a theater lobby.

III-20. In this bronze grill from the Circle Tower Building in Indianapolis, leaping gazelles are surrounded by complex geometric patterns.

Even when the stylized symbolism of Deco design was neither specifically animal nor plant, the symmetrical forms were retained. Many designs in lobbies throughout the country suggested burgeoning nature without specific details, as in this detail of the Wiltern Theater in Los Angeles.

III-23. A symmetrical ornamental panel from the Wiltern Theater uses abstracted nature motifs that seem to grow upward in a carefully controlled sequence.

The Human Body

The human body, either personifying the forces of nature (as we have seen), or in the guise of an ancient God or Goddess, was a primary subject for ornamentation and sculpture. Just as the basic design elements in Art Deco form a contrast between the rigid geometry of early modernism and the graceful arcs derived from Art Nouveau, images of the human body fall roughly into two categories (produced simultaneously): the geometric formalism influenced by early modern art, and the more graceful, curving forms derived from classical antiquity and Art Nouveau.

The Stylized Figure

The modernist-influenced human figure, almost robot-like in its stylization, appears primarily in wall reliefs. These strongly stylized images complimented decorative wall designs; the forms were sharp-edged and angular, suggesting both the machine age and dynamic power with their harsh robotic images and impersonal features.

The stylized human figure, often wearing ancient looking dress, had a prominent place on many Deco walls. These figures were often mythical (or pseudo-mythical) gods or heroes of the Classical era. Many personified elemental forces or nature or symbolized scientific knowledge, discovery, or industry. There was little effort to distinguish between Biblical and Greek, Aztec and Egyptian.

III-24 (left) & III-25 (above). Two reliefs by sculptor René Chambellan at the Chanin Building show the stylized, modernist, almost robot-like figures ornamenting the lobby. They were part of a group called "New York—City of Opportunity," symbolizing the spirit of industry. They were combined with abstract motifs.

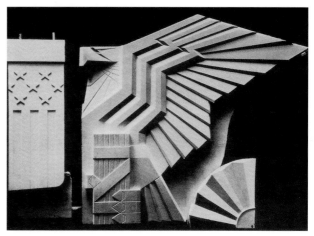

III-26. Sculptor Paul Jennewein's American eagle relief from the Federal Office Building in New York displays a similarly modernistic, geometric style.

Repetition of forms (in many cases, bodies) was common. Many included traditional symbols representing light, water, or other natural forces. These human figures were both decorative and expressive of the optimistic Deco era, picturing, for example, a glowing candle symbolizing light and knowledge.

III-27. In a bas relief from the former Bullock's Department Store in Los Angeles, repeated, stylized, profiled figures offer a symbolic candle of illumination.

Some Deco human figures featured more graceful figures. Bronze female forms in more humanistic poses suggesting a kind of updated antiquity were also typical of the Deco period. These lithe, well-proportioned figures were generally posed in dynamic motion, or controlling nature. Flowing scarves and dress drapery added to the sense of movement— as if the figures were captured in the midst of wind-tossed activity. Sometimes exotic-looking beings added another decorative and symbolic element.

III-28. These elevator doors made of nickel and brass are from the First National City Trust Company Building in New York. The more rounded symmetrical figures kneel before an abstract pattern.

III-29. A series of more realistic symbolic figures adorn the Pantages Theater in Los Angeles, one of the most elaborate Deco theaters in the country.

The use of the human body in Deco imagery expanded into the world of sculpture. The building boom of the 1920s and 1930s created wide opportunities to American sculptors. No interior was thought complete without an allegorical or classical-seeming sculpture as part of it. Particular mythological figures—for example, Diana with her greyhound, were popular elements in the Deco setting.

As freestanding sculpture became more and more common, various American artists received commissions for public buildings, and cast numerous copies of smaller sculptures for public purchase. The graceful symbolic figure became an integral part of the Deco interior. The most notable sculptor both before 1925 and after, was Paul Manship, whose work was considered sufficiently "modern" to appeal to the new era, but not so abstract as to offend conservative American taste. Working within nature's forms, he created a style characterized by a kind of streamlined, modernized antiquity with references to ancient Minoan and Greek art. His graceful female figures appeared to be "caught" in suspended motion (another tribute to Deco's emphasis on movement)—often with a dog or fawn in tandem. His works were thought to be ideal for public spaces, among them Rockefeller Center in New York, where his Prometheus was prominently displayed.

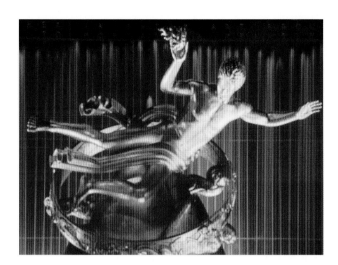

III-32. Like many of Manship's works, "Prometheus," a New York landmark at Rockefeller Center, combined archaic Greek mythology with the Deco emphasis on movement and surface elegance.

Other American sculptors whose work captured the Deco aesthetic included Edward McCartan, Paul Jennewein, Alan Clark, and Harriet Frishmuth. Their works, often in polished bronze, suggested Deco sensibilities, as well as the continuing fascination of the time with ancient mythology. In almost all cases the faces in their sculptures were generalized or anonymous.

William Zorach was somewhat more daring; his "Spirit of the Dance" was commissioned by Radio City Music Hall for its Art Deco interior, was rejected as shocking, and then after public outcry, returned to the building as an integral part of the décor.

III-30 & III-31. The many works of sculptor Paul Manship, who created "Flight of Night" (above left), 1916, and "Dancer with Gazelles" (above right) predated and then came to epitomize the eclectic, graceful style of American Deco era sculpture.

III-33. "Diana with a Hound" by Edward McCartan, whose work of the 1920s and 1930s included many different versions of the Greek goddess with a hound or deer.

III-34. Paul Jennewein's "Greek Dancer" (c. 1925-26) showed his interest in mythology, perfect balance, and graceful line; works like this were reproduced numerous times and placed in Deco interiors.

III-35. During the Deco era Harriet Frishmuth created dozens of small female figures in shiny bronze with deliberate charm; their theme was usually dancing motion.

III-36. William Zorach's "Spirit of the Dance" for Radio City Music Hall was briefly rejected before public outcry brought it back.

The Exotic Figure

American Deco sculptors and designers also recreated the exotic styles of Asia and the ancient Americas, mixing and matching motifs with ease. Like the more abstract motifs borrowed from the Egyptian or Aztec or ancient Greece, sculpted human figures revealed a combination of archaic and exotic traits, often surrounded by typically Deco symmetry, curlicues, and parallel wavy stripes.

III-37. Metal design from the renovated landmark Netherlands Plaza (now the Hilton Hotel) in Cincinnati presents a stylized, exotic figure of a woman surrounded by decorative plants and curlicues; it epitomized the Deco aesthetic.

III-38. Alan Clark's "Balinese Dancer" of 1927 shows how exoticism was adopted by some American sculptors of the Deco period.

III-39. A copper, aluminum, chrome, bronze, steel, and enamel plaque at Rockefeller Center represents Comedy and Tragedy; its three figures are characteristic of the Deco era in their suggestion of Greek myth, the anonymity of their faces, the mixture of exotic materials, styles, and imagery, and their emphasis on the female body.

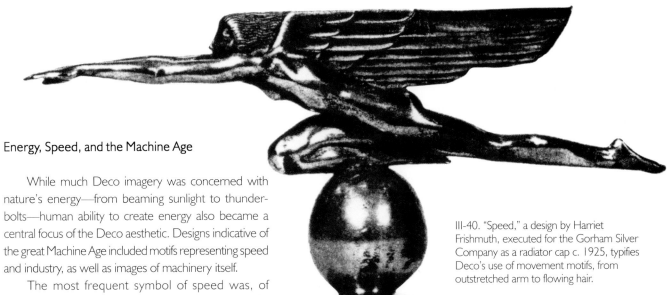

Energy, Speed, and the Machine Age

While much Deco imagery was concerned with nature's energy—from beaming sunlight to thunderbolts—human ability to create energy also became a central focus of the Deco aesthetic. Designs indicative of the great Machine Age included motifs representing speed and industry, as well as images of machinery itself.

The most frequent symbol of speed was, of course, flight: the flying bird and, eventually, the airplane became familiar motifs. As representative of speed and freedom, the soaring bird with its leaning, outstretched form, can be found in all kinds of Deco venues. Sometimes the speeding figure is a human form in full motion, with hair and scarves rippling in the wind. Parallel wavy lines also symbolized speed and motion; they suggested both currents of air and the motion of the water. Various motifs of birds included both the image of the bird and rippling lines to indicate its speed.

Speed stripes, in fact, became a common symbol, with or without the flying bird or plane. Such parallel stripes, borrowed perhaps from Egyptian design, were widely and exuberantly used to suggest motion, as well as to provide striking decoration. The newly popular radio became another source of design, with symbolic radio waves represented by flashes and zigzags and parallel rays of light.

III-40. "Speed," a design by Harriet Frishmuth, executed for the Gorham Silver Company as a radiator cap c. 1925, typifies Deco's use of movement motifs, from outstretched arm to flowing hair.

III-41. The cover of a 1930 "Dance" magazine emphasizes speed and motion, with contrasting diagonals and windswept hair and drapery.

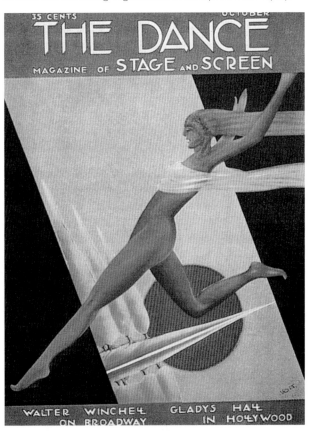

III-42. This design from the Chanin Building is part of a terracotta and bronze frieze using birds and wave motifs to indicate motion.

The Machine

In addition, machine part motifs, like cogged wheels and gears, were used by architects, artists, and metal designers both as artistic and symbolic forms. When combined with such abstract images as zigzags and parallel stripes these machine parts suggested a heady mixture of motion and the attractions of machinery and dynamic power.

Machine parts became a fixture of various Deco design, typified by the automotive imagery used by the Chrysler Company building in New York, which actually included overlapping car motifs on the spire, a frieze of hub-caps and mudguards made of monel-metal, and winged radiator cap gargoyles on the exterior. Buildings decorated with various machine parts acted as advertisements for industrial progress.

III-43. Black and white stripe motif and gold parallel stripes in the lobby of the Film Center Building show how horizontal stripes were another way Deco designers suggested movement and interior excitement.

III-44. Sculptor René Chambellan designed this gate in the Chanin Building; it features a variety of machine images, including gears and wheels, as well as more abstract representations of power and motion.

Other building designers (as well as artists) also found the abstract beauty of machine parts interesting, creating designs that were both attractive and symbolic of the industry of the company for which they were built. The Central Heating and Refrigeration Plant in Washington, for example, included a sculptural panel drawn from their own machinery.

The interest in the aesthetic pleasures of machines coincided with mass production, and the idea that an inexpensive material like plastic could be considered fashionable was a new element. Deco was the first style to reach down to popular taste, and in response, a market was created for mass production. Thus the machine aesthetic and mass production became irrevocably linked as Art Deco became the first style to end an age-old conflict between art and industry.

III-45. Detail of the decoration at the Central Heating and Refrigeration Plant in Washington, c. 1933-1934 features abstract images of machinery and makes function into an art form.

Transportation and Travel

Transportation and travel became subjects for Deco design, as well. In addition to Chrysler's automotive motifs, images of planes, ships, and trains became popular. Murals and sculpture featured rushing vehicles spewing clouds of steam, often accompanied by the parallel wavy lines that were Deco shorthand for speed. The great Deco ceiling fresco at Bullock's Department Store in Los Angeles included steamships, airplanes, and trains, all surrounded with stylized puffs of smoke and rippling waves. Similarly, the W.P.A. mural at Omaha's Union Pacific Station shows a train arriving under a skyline of parallel wavy lines suggesting motion.

III-47. A Works Progress Administration mural in Omaha—one of many in public buildings across the country—celebrates transportation. The parallel wavy lines suggest motion.

III-46. A detail of the brilliant ceiling fresco in what was once Bullock's Department Store in Los Angeles has as its subject transportation, including boats, trains, and flight, as seen here.

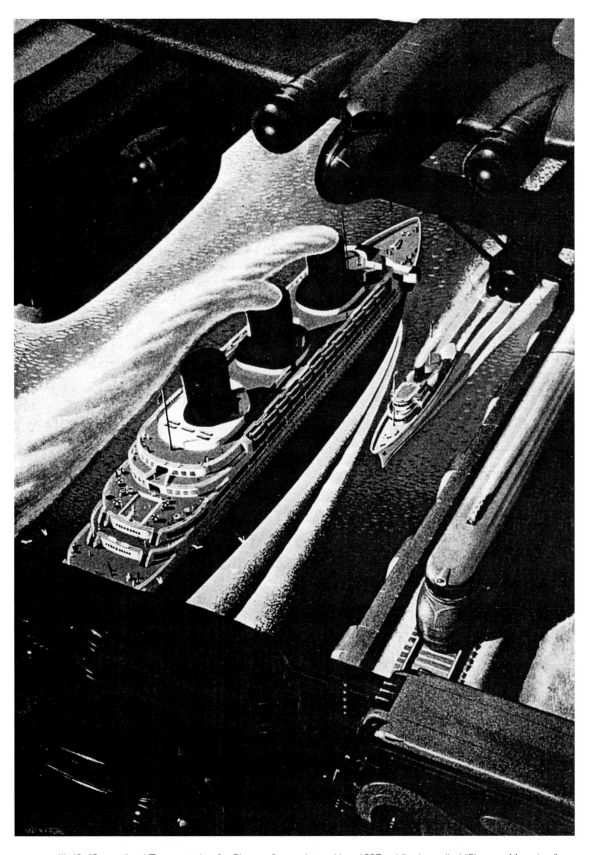

III-48. "Streamlined Transportation for Pleasure" was pictured in a 1937 publication called "Pleasure Magazine."

Radio Waves and Electricity

Radio waves, indicated by similarly parallel, lightning-like flashes or zigzags, appeared too—typically as ornament on a radio of the Deco era. Like the speed of airplane travel, the unseen waves of the radio were images that captured the era's fascination with vibrancy, motion, and speed. Even sulpted birds took on the metallic machine forms in art of the period.

III-49. Parallel, wavy lines were also used to indicate radio waves, as seen in this 1930s wireless design.

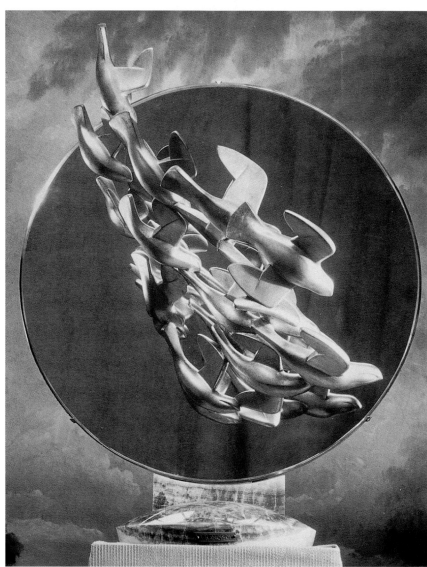

III-50. "Birds in Flight," a sculpture by Anthony De Francisi in 1936, shows the influence of machine forms and materials on a natural subject.

These elements of speed and travel and energy, like so many other Deco motifs, were positive, upbeat reflections of the new age. For these themes represented a central facet of American Deco: optimism. Images like these, they seemed to say, show how positive are the relationships between man, nature, and machinery—all controlled by human hands.

III-51

III-51 & III-52. Two recently renovated sections of the illuminated glass panels at the Mohawk Power Company in Syracuse represent the Deco era's optimistic and stylized take on the generation and transmission of electric power.

III-52

THE MATERIALS

American Deco interiors were characterized by a rich and eclectic collection of materials. Some were derived from European Deco, like the emphasis on glass and polished wood; others were influenced by industrial materials, such as monel-metal and aluminum. Often in strikingly deep colors or dramatic black and white, these interiors were among the most richly ornamented in history. The unusual mixing of materials, including mosaics, tiling, cast plaster, stained glass, wood veneers, patterned fabrics, metalwork, theatrical lighting, mosaics, and murals created an unusual charm and interest in the Deco interior. In addition, furniture and decorative objects featuring exotic materials and patterns added to the overall ambience of each Deco interior. A look at the new handling of the materials of the American Deco era shows both the imagination of designers and the vast array of decorative features in a Deco interior.

Light, Lighting, and Glass

The Deco interior was particularly noteworthy for its emphasis on light and color. Light, both natural and electric, was often the central element that made the Deco interior a fully designed, comprehensive unit. Few previous architectural styles utilized such variety or so involved the lighting system in the overall design of the room. And as the visual arts played such a significant role in the Deco interior, art made of glass and electric light itself, added to the modern look, the illusion of space, and the welcoming atmosphere that so attracted people to the Deco interior.

Throughout the Deco setting this accent on light—whether natural or seemingly so—was dependent on the use of glass. Clear glass was etched, sandblasted, or embossed in geometric patterns. Stained glass—with typically Deco designs—was resurrected. The use of glass panels, mirrored walls, and glass bricks opened up rooms to more light and to interestingly stylized fixtures that were carefully related to the room's design. The combining of translucent and frosted glass also added interest in the Deco interior.

Leading Glass Designers

Both Louis Comfort Tiffany and Frank Lloyd Wright were influential in making glass design an important element of the Deco interior. Tiffany introduced subtle variations in color and linear design. But it was the venerable Wright who brought a form of geometric modernism to American glass design. In windows, walls, and lighting fixtures Wright established geometric design as a complement to his architectural innovations. His use of glass influenced generations of designers to make light an integral part of interior design.

III-53. Wright's 1927 stained glass window for the Biltmore Hotel in Arizona feature an abstract geometric pattern.

III-53

III-54 & III-55. Two early examples of Frank Lloyd Wright's interest in abstract glass design include a "sumac" window and a glass door with lighting fixtures from the Dana-Thomas House.

III-54

Wright taught designers to choose window shapes that contributed geometric interest to the interior. Thus the shape of the windows of the Deco period, following his rigorous aesthetic, tended to reinforce the overall design of the building. Tall, vertical Deco buildings often had long window bays, while those in the horizontal, streamlined style used low horizontal windows to accent their lines. Portholes and triangular windows were also used as design elements.

At the Chrysler Building in New York, the imaginatively used glass added to the overall design. The large window over the transom added to the glamour of the building, accenting its verticality, and decorating the interior with its geometric design of angular panes, and even zigzags.

At Cranbrook, the Michigan art center where the great Finnish designer Eero Saarinen and his colleagues worked with every aspect of design, windows were also a focus of innovation. Large areas were devoted to glass and allowed a maximum of natural light; at the same time a variety of geometric designs kept the glass areas interesting and decorative.

III-56. The door glass from the lobby of the Kingswood Auditorium at Cranbrook uses repeated geometric motifs.

III-57. A glass wall from the lobby at Kingswood Auditorium at Cranbrook features delicately ornamented glass that replicates the geometric patterns on grillwork nearby.

III-58. The great window at the Chrysler Building echoes Deco lobby interior with geometric design and zigzags.

Stained Glass in the Deco Era

Stained glass remained popular throughout the Deco era, both for residential and commercial buildings. But the stained glass panel was not only used for windows. Doors, skylights, and even room partitions were decorated with stained glass in geometric and other stylized motifs. Hildreth Meière's stained glass windows commissioned by St. Bartholomew's Church in New York show how the Deco imagery permeated another aspect of the Deco look.

III-59 & III-60. Hildreth Meière designed the clerestory windows at St. Bartholomew's Church in New York, beginning in 1930; his modernist version of stained glass combines stylized figures and geometric patterns.

III-59

III-60

New Uses for Glass

Windows were not the only way that light was admitted—and indeed celebrated—in the Deco interior. Glass bricks or blocks were building materials that allowed light throughout an entire wall. A new design addition was illumination from behind the glass brick wall, creating a warm, inviting glow. A similar innovation was the mirrored wall, segmented into geometric designs, such as that seen in the Barbizon Plaza Hotel in New York. The complex design of mirrors added a reflective and ever changing decoration to the interior. In some buildings blue, black, or frosted glass mirrors were used for accent.

As the use of glass was expanded by Deco designers, it became a dramatic architectural statement—as it is today in many contemporary interiors. Typical of the original and dynamic use were the spectacular architectural fixtures that decorated many notably Deco public rooms.

III-61. Glass brick became a fashionable building material, allowing both light and delicate brick pattern to cover walls, as in this example from a Bloomingdale's bar pictured in 1935.

III-62. The Barbizon Plaza Hotel made use of mirrors to create a stunningly fragmented lobby design.

Great lighted columns and "fountains of light" were installed in the center of the interior, and ceilings and walls became settings for abstract glass designs. This emphasis on glowing light provided a welcoming warmth, as well as an updated, chic, architectural setting.

As we have seen, the great French glass designer, René Lalique, was a pioneer in using glass as a surface for art and a part of room décor. In his hands, glass became a luminous surface for etching and other design elements. American glass designers were quick to follow.

III-63. A Madison Avenue building in New York displayed a fluted column of light.

III-64. A "Fountain of Light" set in a geometrically ornamented glass panel was part of the Deco design of Oakland's Paramount Theater.

III-65. American glass designer Maurice Heaton celebrated both the romance of flight and the modern use of glass as a pictorial element, by creating the glass mural "Amelia Earhart Crossing the Atlantic" (RKO Roxy Theater in New York).

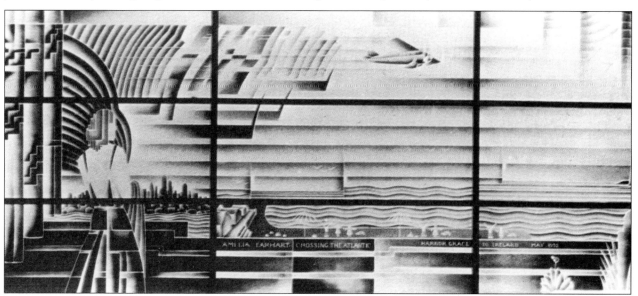

Lighted panels provided surfaces for art, both abstract and symbolic. Entire walls were decorated with glass "murals." American designers like Maurice Heaton created these glass designs, as well as objets d'art of modern glass. His illuminated "Amelia Earhart Crossing the Atlantic" mural for Rockefeller Center was one of the most notable of these new glass murals.

Smaller decorative panels, some of them illuminated, became a major source of design for the Deco interior. Some bore typically Deco designs, like the familiar leaping fawn and plant motifs on a lighting grill from the steamship "Andrea Doria," created by the Steuben Glass Company in 1935. Others used a more abstract approach, such as the illuminated intaglio design in crystal glass, used in 1931 in the Empire State Building. This design was repeated many times, but every other one was inverted, to create an unusual rhythmic sequence.

III-66. A cast lead glass lighting grill, circa 1931, was made by Steuben Glass for the steamship Andrea Doria, with a traditionally Deco leaping gazelle.

III-67. A polished lead glass lighting panel from the elevator lobby of the Empire State Building of 1931 included both geometric and plant motifs.

Sometimes the glass panel was designed as a stunning reminder of the times. In one example from the interior of an elevator, the Manhattan skyline is painted on silver and black, mirrored glass. The false ceiling above this glass painting is made of frosted glass and banded with aluminum; it is illuminated from above.

III-68. Mirrored glass design from the interior of a New York elevator concealed elevator lighting with frosted glass and aluminum pictures of the Manhattan skyline.

Deco Light

And then there were the lighting fixtures themselves, certainly among the most notable and identifiable elements of the Art Deco interior. Combining glass and filigree metal, Deco lighting fixtures helped to create the characteristic aura associated with the Deco "look." Overhead fixtures and wall lamps picked up the geometric elements of the surrounding décor, and the combinations of repeated motifs and interlocking glass and metal surfaces lent them a new and dramatic look. The light cast by such illuminated ceilings was warm and welcoming.

Lighting fixtures had always imitated architectural styles; in the Deco interior a combination of the emphasis on electric light and the technical expertise of the industry made lighting ever more important and appealing to designers. Here was a design medium that had hardly been explored before—just waiting for a variety of innovative decorative uses. While later designers may have tried to disguise the source of electric light, those of the Deco era reveled in it, using all manner of globes, motifs, and original fixtures to add to the overall ambience of the room. Many architects, following Wright's lead, designed their own lighting for interiors. Using a wide variety of materials—tubular steel, plastics, aluminum, brass, pressed glass, chrome, and acrylic, and even plywood, enabled designers to produce a wide variety of lighting fixtures.

Reflections, from the various metal elements in the room, as well as from window and electric light, became positive additions to the room. Niches, hanging lights with metallic decoration, large globes, and other innovations made lighting central to the décor. Large circles and domes in ceilings created reflective power, as in the Cranbrook Auditorium in Michigan, and in the ceiling of the Daily News Building in New York.

Recessed lighting added subtle warmth to the room, and dozens of differently styled wall sconces were designed to fit within the niches.

III-69. Ceilings became an additional design site; repeated light fixtures created a ceiling pattern of circles to decorate an interior at Kingswood, Cranbrook.

III-70. The ceiling of the lobby of the Daily News Building in New York was an integral part of the overall design with its shiny reach of black glass, geometric pattern, and central globe.

Neon lighting, too, became popular, particularly in tropical climates and nightspots throughout the country. Neon, in slender tubes, added a modernistic or geometric touch. Sometimes, it too was recessed behind ceiling panels or used to accent staircases or other architectural features. It was during the Deco era that resorts discovered that pulsating neon light created an atmosphere of heady excitement.

Openly opulent chandeliers and repeated ceiling lights also created a romantic aura. (This romanticism was sometimes embellished by the use of pink or rose-toned lights.) The combination of wall and ceiling ornamentation with lighting created a profoundly new atmosphere within the Deco room. Hanging lights and wall sconces were prominent as well, imitating and complementing the geometric interaction of straight and curving lines. Many lobbies of the great Deco buildings in American cities were illuminated with fanciful hanging lights and distinguished wall sconces. Even the shadows cast by these lights lent interesting patterns to the tiling or wall designs around them. Their forms ranged from ziggurats to cones, flowers to heavenly bodies—and many were additionally etched or patterned with Deco motifs. Wall lighting also offered designers the opportunity to create ornamental sconces and unusual architectural statements through light.

Overhead Deco lighting fixtures allowed designers free play with shapes and materials:

III-72. Chanin Building, New York

III-71. 275 Madison Avenue, New York

III-73. Wiltern Theater, Los Angeles

III-74. Former Bullock's Department Store, Los Angeles

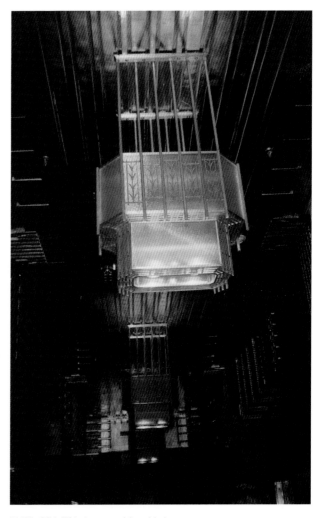

III-75. 251 Fifth Avenue, New York

III-76. 2 Park Avenue, New York

III-77. Repeated overhead fixtures with a central circle decorate "Hall of Mirrors" in the elegant refurbished former Cincinnati Netherlands Plaza Hotel (now the Hilton).

III-78 through III-81. Wall fixtures offered designers an opportunity to extend architectural interest throughout the interior, both by making the fixture itself a miniature architectural statement, and by the use of decorative metal detailing.

III-78. New York apartment building

III-79. Wiltern Theater, Los Angeles

III-80. New York Central Railroad Station, Buffalo

III-81. General Bronze Corporation,
American National Bank Building, Chicago

A glass panel from the 1930s epitomizes the major strands of Deco design. One of the single largest pieces created by René Lalique (who did a number of commissions for the United States between 1928 and 1935), it was a graceful sandblasted cut glass panel for Wanamaker's in Philadelphia. Its stylized figure beneath a leaf tree reflected the motifs and grace of so much Deco art and design.

III-82. The 1932 Lalique glass panel for the entrance lobby of Wanamaker's Department Store in Philadelphia demonstrates the elegance provided by Deco glass design.

Another pair of panels from the Mohawk Power Company in Syracuse show us the Machine Age in glass: two of the four brilliant illuminated glass panels represent different aspects of light and power. Here, in a "temple of electricity" are "Gas" and "Illumination," as symbolically described in glass that was lighted at night. The panel entitled Illumination, in fact, was meant to picture the "city of the future."

III-83

III-83 & III-84. The illuminated glass panels of the Mohawk Power and Light in Syracuse celebrated power, industry and modernity.

III-84

Wood

One of the most appealing aspects (to our modern eye) of the Art Deco interior was the use of wood—indeed, many woods. From ebony (Art Deco's favorite for furniture) to intersecting panels of cherry wood and maple, wood became a prime surface and decorative element. Even pine and other less expensive woods were used to ornament interior walls and floors. Veneers became very popular. While darker woods were favored for walls, highly polished pale wood was the chosen surface for the Deco floor. In keeping with the interest in ornamentation throughout the interior, many such surfaces were designed in parquet patterns. Polished, and often lighted by the ubiquitous wall sconces and overhead fixtures of their time, wood surfaces and veneers gleamed brightly, adding to the glowing, inviting tones of the room. The wood-walled interior became a symbol of luxury and elegance. Most often highly polished or veneered, the deep toned elegance of the surface made a statement of richness and sophistication.

Typical of the emphasis on highly polished wood tones was the private office above Radio City Music Hall, designed for the manager by Donald Deskey. Paneled cherry wood walls and a reflective gilded ceiling, with accents of glass and shiny metal, created an environment suggesting luxury and warmth. Lacquer, which was rediscovered in the 1920s, became another element that added to the bright and shining interior favored by Deco designers.

III-85. Warmed-tone cherry wood paneling decorated the interior of chic private office above Radio City Music Hall; it was designed by Donald Deskey.

In the great skyscrapers of the era wood was also used in elevator interiors, and in door and lobby design. Squares, triangles, and curves formed contrasting patterns, both in shape and wood color. Cubist-inspired design in wood decorated surfaces of all types. The Chrysler Building took the lead; elevator interiors were created like works of art. One had a stunning design of intersecting squares in different woods, while the other featured an Egyptian-inspired pattern of stylized lotus flowers that simultaneously suggested the overlapping industrial images on the building's tower.

III-86 & III-87. Both Cubist and Egyptian influences are evident in the wood-veneered interiors of two of the elevators in the Chrysler Building.

III-86

III-87

III-88 & III-89. Polished wood moldings and gilded wood ornaments were popular design elements, as in the Suffolk Theater of the early 1930s.

In many interiors wood became a rhythmic accent in an otherwise painted interior. The 1930s Suffolk Theater lobby shows how polished geometric and step-shaped decorations gave the interior its character. At the top of each thin column, with its parallel vertical lines, a gold-leafed ornamentation echoed the gilded decorations on the walls. Contrasting plain and delicately decorated wood added a sense of intimacy to the interior. Typical of the Deco aesthetic was the use of parallel stripes (sometimes known as speed stripes) combined with ornate filigree and flower designs.

III-90. Elaborately carved wood designs, in Deco's customary plant motifs, added to the glamour of the Wiltern Theater's lobby.

As the emphasis on streamline design became more pronounced, newer materials were added to the wood décor. Frequently wood became a background to such recent materials as bakelite and chrome, with the rich tones of wood forming a striking contrast with the chic metallic accents. The elevator doors in Bullock's Wilshire resemble an abstract painting; their wooden surface accented by brass, gunmetal, and copper. The eating alcove at a small restaurant in Baltimore combined chrome with wood veneer for an updated, chic look.

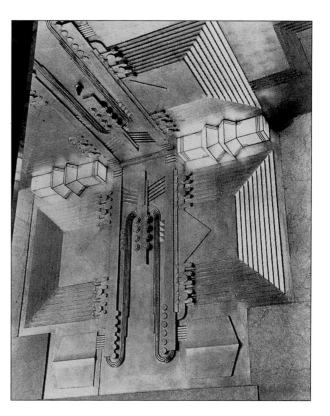

III-91

III-91 & III-92. Complicated molding resembling modernist sculpture as well as skyscrapers themselves, created architectural interest in a Ely Jacques Kahn Building, and in the Barclay Vesey Building, both in New York.

III-92

III-93. Elevator doors of Deco landmarks were often made of wood with accents of metal, as in this example from the former Bullocks Department Store in Los Angeles. Its detailing is in brass, copper, and gunmetal.

Some designers chose to color their wood designs. Polychromed surfaces used both carving and color, creating painting-like doors or wall décor as a major design element of the interior. A typical example were sculptor Lee Lawrie's design for faux-Egyptian doors for the Senate Chamber of the Nebraska State Capitol, made around 1934.

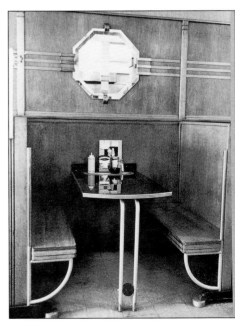

III-94. A booth in a Baltimore restaurant called Verner's combined glossy wood-pattern formica with accents of newly fashionable chrome and Bakelite.

III-95. Wood was sometimes colored as well as carved; these polychrome doors by sculptor Lee Lawrie gave the Nebraska State Capitol a touch of Egyptian design.

Plaster and Terra Cotta

Wood was not the only material called upon to add to the decorative aspects of the style. Plaster, that most plebeian of building materials, and terra cotta, one of the most decorative, took on new dimensions in Deco design. Like wood, plaster and terra cotta became mediums for complicated patterning on ceilings and walls. Terra cotta remained primarily an exterior design material, with occasional indoor use. But plaster's use ranged from astonishingly complex motifs adorning ceilings and walls of grand movie palaces to delicate moldings and sculptural forms. Inventiveness, and an eye for Cubist-like design, led to complex geometric patterning on many surfaces, as well as imaginative flights of fancy.

Sometimes painted in brilliant colors or gilded, plaster designs gave interiors a form of dramatic built-in art. Patterns included the typically geometric to a characteristic Deco amalgam of the exotic—with motifs suggesting perhaps the Aztec, Egyptian or Babylonian motifs. An example can be seen in the lobby of the Film Center Building designed by Jacques Ely Kahn; here gilded, molded plaster appears in pyramid shapes and horizontal stripes to create a brilliantly decorative interior. Another example is the ceiling of the Wiltern Theater in Los Angeles.

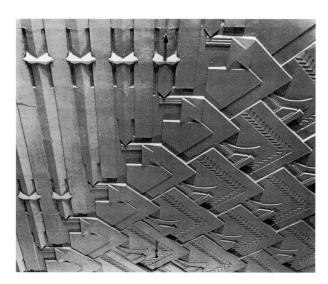

III-96. Molded plaster ceiling of a 1928 Kahn and Buchman Building in New York shows how inventively designers used the most mundane of materials.

III-97. A detail of a molded eagle and geometric ceiling design from a New York building suggests a coat-of-arms.

III-98 & III-99. The elaborately designed walls and ceiling of the Wiltern Theater in Los Angeles combines round and straight elements in a dynamic diagonal design, as well as plant patterns.

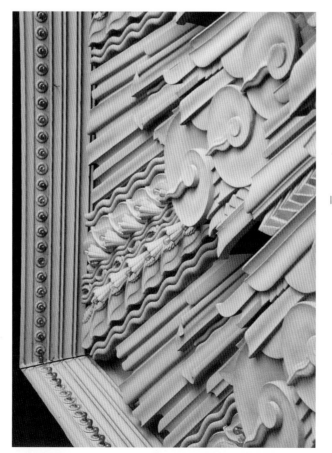

III-98

III-100 & III-101. Kahn's 1928-29 Film Center lobby in New York used large amounts of gold, with horizontal stripes of molded plaster in stepped pyramid shapes.

III-101

122

Metal

Art Deco's ornamental elements were often created by elaborate metalwork. The complex and free-spirited use of grills and decorative screens and even entire walls made of various metals created interiors that glowed with polished, lacy surfaces. Repetition of various motifs was typical, with similar patterns paced throughout an interior. In fact, no element of Deco design is more characteristic, and more easily spotted, in buildings of the twenties and thirties.

Like calligraphy in art, metalwork enabled designers of an interior to create linear patterns that created both contrast and accent in an area. The freedom and complexity of many of these ornamental designs is astonishing. In architecture, which is not often characterized by delicate linear surface patterns, such metalwork areas added elegance and glamour, as well as occasional symbolic messages.

Decorative metalwork was used in everything from elevator doors to air ducts, window grates to fire screens. It provided a polished decorative setting for mail slots, a repeated accent for windows and lighting, and a glowing, reflective surface to complement wood and other materials.

III-103

III-102 & III-103. Mail box and wall design from the Wiltern Theater in Los Angeles, and 1931 air duct from the former Juilliard School (now the Manhattan School of Music) show how decorative metalwork could ornament the most common features of a building.

III-102

The metal grill was usually created of wrought iron or bronze, but other, newly fashionable metals were used too. Artisans bent and twisted the molten metal into sinuous forms that often suggested ancient and exotic arts, occasionally featuring a goddess-like figure or leaping gazelle amid the curving forms and abstracted shapes of vines and waves. Typically elegant was the Edgar Brandt design for the Cheney Building.

III-104. Edgar Brandt was America's leading metal designer; his elegant doors for the Cheney Brothers Building featured a charming wrought iron design with details of gilt-bronze fountain at the top.

Doorways and entrances became the show place for many Deco buildings; the theatricality of an ornate doorway beckoned the visitor into the interior. Designer Edgar Brandt's elegant doors for the Cheney Brothers Building in new York featured wrought iron flowers with a gilt-bronze fountain; the decorative door itself was an invitation to enter the building.

Grill work in lobbies and other public spaces was characterized by remarkably complex, usually symmetrical patterns. Frequently divided into small rectangular units, these designs were playful and repetitive, featuring symmetrical abstract pattern intermingled with symbolic forms that suggested nature: sunbursts, waves, and blooming flowers. Some of the most dramatic metal work had designs with cosmic overtones. Using repeated parallel lines in upward sweeps, these pictorial metal "pictures" suggested grand natural forces, like bursts of sun and wind. In the ever-taller buildings of New York and Chicago, for example, rising, elongated shapes were common. Each example was a piece of art in itself, although it had a nominal duty as a radiator cover or wall panel.

The Chanin Building in New York used highly decorative metalwork. Radiator grills include abstract ziggurat shaped designs, while another features a series of natural plant forms with parallel curving motifs that suggest burgeoning growth and dynamic energy, and a third shows the dynamic curves and lines of cosmic dynamism.

III-105. The parallel strips of metalwork at 630 Fifth Avenue in New York feature symmetry and leaf-like forms.

III-106 through III-109. Abstract, decorative grill designs from New York buildings typify Deco metal detailing with their combination of symmetry and free form.

III-105. 261 Fifth Avenue

125

III-107. Chanin Building

III-109. Chanin Building

III-108. Chanin Building

Entrances to elevators became focal points for many tall building lobbies, providing designers with a perfect "canvas" on which to display the Deco idiom. The vertical shape of the doors gave the designer the opportunity to play with long lines, diagonals and other geometric patterns, sometimes continuing the design above the doors themselves. The step motif, the triangle, and Native-American design were typical, as were the glamorous, subtly ancient goddess-like figures on the elevator doors of a Chicago building.

III-111. Simply, but elegantly ornamented elevator at 275 Madison Avenue, New York

III-110. Polished bronze elevator from the Central Bronze Corp. in Chicago

III-110 through III-113. Elevators were especially prominent in Deco lobby design. Made of a variety of different metals, including highly polished brass, elevators became central to the building's interior design, rather than merely utilitarian.

III-112. Brass design above a double-decker elevator at 60 Wall Street, New York

Frequently metalwork was combined with glass to create a more transparent image. The great bronze and glass partition in the Union Company of Detroit is one example. Made for a bank, this partition not only created a protective wall, but had a notable intricacy of design and ornamentation.

III-113. The ultimate Deco elevator graced lobby at Union Trust Company in Detroit; it was made of fashionable incised monel metal, inset with Tiffany glass, and framed in Numidian red marble in a typically Deco pyramid shape.

III-114. Bronze was combined with glass in this ornate gate from the Standard Savings and Loan, Union Company of Detroit.

And then there were the entire walls and ceilings made of ornamental metalwork. Primarily used in movie palaces of the thirties, these stunning displays were the height of Deco excessiveness, nonetheless expressing grandeur, artistry, and a fanciful elegance. The Wiltern Theater in Los Angeles had column after column of glorious grillwork interspersed with plain vertical panels—all of it richly glowing and inviting. With characteristic patterns from nature rising ever higher, the vertical sweep of both the architecture and the intricate patterning created a brilliant wall of ornament.

III-115. The walls of the Wiltern Theater alternated plain vertical stripes with strips of elaborate metallic ornament.

When an entire room was ornamented with lacy metal-work, the result could be overwhelming. The décor of the Fox-Wilshire, also in Los Angeles, featured the most fanciful use of metal grillwork imaginable in its day, with lacy patterns surfacing both ceilings and walls like a giant wedding cake.

In the former Netherlands Plaza Hotel in Cincinnati (now the Hilton and recently renovated), decorative grillwork in its reception room extends from walls and ceilings to railings, frames, fixtures, and panels. Each element has its own ornamental design, giving the room a calligraphic elegance. Many of the traditional Art Deco images are combined in the one interior, with somewhat dazzling effect.

III-116. Like many picture palaces, the Fox-Wiltshire (1930) in Los Angeles used the most fanciful decorations they could devise—in this case metallic Deco meshwork.

III-117. Refurbished interior at Cincinnati landmark 1931 Netherlands Plaza Hotel (now the Hilton) shows how many decorative uses metal could have in the elaborately redone interior.

PICTORIAL IMAGES EVERYWHERE

No element is more characteristic of the Deco interior than the intersection of the arts, and in particular, the use of built-in art to cover walls. Thus, murals, reliefs, mosaics, and other types of wall decoration can be found in all kinds of Deco settings—including private homes, public theaters, and sky-scraper lobbies. The Art Deco era brought back into fashion a variety of media—from fresco to mosaics—that had not been so widely used since the Renaissance.

Artfully painted walls were central to the original Deco interiors of France. As we have seen, climbing tree branches and ornamental flowers decorated walls, while the more daring rooms included painted or architectural stripes. In the United States there was a resurgence of mural painting. From the walls of the Bullock's Department Store in Los Angeles to the ceiling of the Chrysler Building and the halls of Rockefeller Center in New York, murals were a sign of the new age.

Wall decoration was often added to rooms that were already painted with rich and vibrant wall color; most popular were deep blues, vivid purples and mauves, magenta, orange, lime green and bright yellow. Deep silver and a variety of reflective glass and metal surfaces were used to contrast with these rich tones. The combination of brilliant background and additional wall decoration added to the complexity and brilliance of the interior.

Deco Murals and Plaques

By the 1930s in America, murals were everywhere. With the advent of the Works Progress Administration (W.P.A.) a new age of public art brought wall design (as well as other public arts) to post offices, city halls, theaters, building lobbies, schools, and many other American buildings. Needless to say, many of the murals were influenced by the Art Deco style.

Such murals and frescos were common to the Deco lobby because they not only carried pictorial messages (speed, transportation, industrial might, the dignity of work, among other symbolic themes), but because they brought art into the very center of interior spaces frequented by many people.

The best-known Art Deco murals in America were surely the ceiling frescos of Bullock's Department Store in Los Angeles. Here a colorful and artistically conceived horizontal plane was covered with a variety of trains, ships, and airplanes, cleverly intertwined with geometrically stylized puffs of smoke, wavy seas, and even a running man. In all, the Bullock's rose-toned ceiling was a stunning and eye-catching addition to the building.

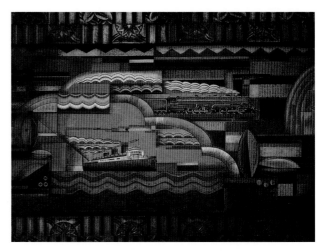

III-118. The painted ceiling of the former Bullock's Department Store celebrated transportation, with images of planes, trains, and ships amid puffs of smoke.

While the popularity of wall paintings was typical of the Deco interior, such murals were painted in many styles by a number of notable artists, who contributed to the popularity of murals in public buildings during the Deco period. Modernist painters were asked to undertake some murals to decorate public buildings, like those in the newly designed Rockefeller Center. Stuart Davis contributed a jazzy, semi-abstract mural for Radio City Music Hall; it featured familiar details of American life (such as a barber pole and a roadster) but gave an overall impression of verve and modernity. Also at Radio City was the sinuous "Crouching Panther" by Henry Billings, its curvy lines contrasting with the geometric furniture and wallpaper surrounding it. A charming mural by John Gabriel Beckman on a wall of the Avalon Theater on Catalina Island had the fanciful quality of the Russian set designs that had originally influenced Art Deco in France.

III-119. The Chrysler Building's distinctive tower was replicated in the lobby with a painted image.

III-120. The stunning, jazzy, semi-abstract mural by American artist Stuart Davis was painted for the Radio City Music Hall's smoking room; the furniture was designed by Donald Deskey.

III-121. Artist Henry Billings designed another mural at Radio City, this one was in the Ladies' Powder Room; called "Crouching Panther," it was surrounded by Deskey furnishings and geometric wallpaper.

III-122. A mural by John Gabriel Beckman was painted on the wall of the auditorium at the Avalon Theater on Catalina Island; its free form and fanciful air are reminiscent of the Russian set design that influenced the French Deco movement.

Some murals were carefully calibrated to their surroundings, with furniture, carpets, and lighting all featuring similar shapes and themes. One of the more fanciful such interiors was the card room of a 1928 club in Chicago, where even the design of the chairs picked up the playing card theme of the murals.

III-123. The card room at the rooftop Tavern Club in Chicago, designed in 1928, combined murals with especially designed furniture to emphasize the symbolism of playing cards.

Sometimes the wall decoration was photographic, rather than painted. Drawing upon the talents of one of the most notable photographers of the day, N.B.C. commissioned Margaret Bourke-White's photomural for their visitor's area at Rockefeller Center. This photographic piece pictured radio transmission equipment in a series of dramatic images.

III-124. Brilliant photo-mural by noted photographer Margaret Bourke-White, showing radio transmission equipment was in the reception hall of the R.C.A. Building in New York.

Wall Reliefs and Plaques

We have already seen the prominent place held by sculpture in the Deco era. Plaques and sculptural wall reliefs (both indoors and out) were also a prominent design element of the period. Large sculptured reliefs were common to skyscrapers, while smaller relief sculptures adorned more intimate spaces. Bronze was used as a pictorial form as well; this plaque celebrates Charles Lindberg's flight and the glories of aviation. Typical of the Deco relief was a Lee Lawrie design for Rockefeller Center. Lawrie, who made the great sculpture of Atlas for the Center, also contributed smaller works, like his bright relief panel with dashing horseman and rearing steed, amidst typically Deco parallel wavy lines and stars.

III-125. Many new types of surfaces were used for pictorial decor. This bronze work celebrating Charles Lindberg's flight was made by George Grey Barnard in 1927.

III-126. Sculpted relief panels were another form of wall decoration in Deco America. Lee Lawrie contributed a number of artworks to Rockefeller Center, including this brightly colored relief with dashing rider, rearing steed, and decorative outlines.

Another sculptured frieze shows a series of silhouetted dancers in a stylized manner popular among some sculptors who eschewed modernism, but did not consider themselves realists either. Among them were John David Brcin, whose "Romanza" was displayed at the Contemporary American Sculpture show in 1929.

III-127. Stone reliefs were increasingly popular, both indoors and out. John David Brcin made this 1929 relief called "Romanza," which features Deco design elements of motion, with parallel figures dancing from antiquity tomodernity.

III-128. Some reliefs were made of metal, like the chromium plated frieze at the former St. George's Hotel in Brooklyn; it combined antique symbolism and modern urbanism.

The chromium-plated frieze brought the sculptural form a new kind of sleek surfacing that also appealed to the much-touted age of industry and energy. The cityscape in chrome that formed part of the décor of Brooklyn's St. George Hotel was typical. Combining realistic images of subway, bus, and skyscraper with symbols of speed and progress, the frieze fits many of the criteria of Deco design.

Mosaics and Tiles

In addition to murals and reliefs, mosaics, which had long been regarded primarily as a liturgical art form, came into new popularity during the Deco age. Created both for abstract design purposes and as a medium for pictorial images, the use of mosaics blossomed during the skyscraper boom. No interior space more dramatically emphasized mosaics than the foyer of the Banking Hall of the Irving Trust Company (1932) in New York. This stunning interior featured a room with exceptionally high ceilings (37 feet), its walls and ceiling fully decorated with reflective Venetian glass mosaics—some 8900 square feet of reds, oranges, and gold pieces with lightning designs.

III-129. As mosaic design made its notable comeback from obscurity, whole walls were covered with tiny pieces of cut glass and other materials. This example of reflective glass mosaic walls is from the foyer of the Banking Hall at the Irving Trust Company in New York.

On a more intimate scale were the mosaic ornamentations in the Film Center Building, also in New York. Here, in the small lobby designed by Ely Jacques Kahn, a brilliant display of red, blue, and gold mosaic contrasted with stunning black and silver stripes. The mosaic design suggested the Aztec, but the overall impression—particularly appropriate to a center for the movie industry—was fantastic, imaginative, outré.

III-130. Brilliant mosaic designs decorated many lobbies like this one at 261 Fifth Avenue in New York.

Tiles, too, had a prominent place in the Deco interior. Tiling was used in a carefree and original way to cover walls, floors, and ceilings, often in giddy profusion and brilliant colors. Like mosaics, tiling became a vehicle for overall decoration, as well as for pictorial additions to the interior. In many cases tile was combined with other decorative elements, as in the examples shown here.

The tile and etched glass bathroom at the Chanin Building produced a bright, modern-looking décor, which used geometric repeated motifs. The glamorous tile and metalwork arch at the Union Trust Building in Detroit was an eye-catching decorative announcement. Its colorful vaulted ceiling was not just an abstract pattern; in fact it represented a beehive (symbolizing both industry and thrift).

III-131. A fully tiled, particularly elegant bathroom in the Chanin Building uses the tiles for geometric designs, including an "Egyptian" sunrise.

III-132. The brightly tiled, marble columned lobby arch at the 1929 Union Trust Company in Detroit, had reflective metal elevators and desks that echo the bright colors of the tiling.

And at the Valencia Hotel in La Jolla not far from Holly-wood, where Art Deco design, movie glamour, and Southern California style blended into a striking mix, a lobby was decorated with stunning tiling. Here, as celebrity culture and Deco design elements intersected, there were both glamorous images of a star and purely abstract motifs in tile and mosaic.

III-133. A ceiling fixture is suspended from a tile design at the former Bullock's Department Store.

III-134

III-134 through III-137. Examples of wall design from La Valencia Hotel in La Jolla, California show the ornamental use of tile and mosaic, both in abstract patterns and glamorous imagery.

III-135

III-136

III-137

149

Flooring and Carpets

Walls and ceilings were not the only setting for design; like other parts of the Deco interior, the floor was also reconsidered. Geometric decoration, with circles, triangles, and complex patterning was commonly used to offset and reflect the other parts of the room. One of the most popular materials for floors was polished terrazzo; decorative motifs included circles and sunbursts and even maps and eagles. Linoleum also became an inexpensive and popular material for flooring. Most Deco floors were highly polished, adding another reflective element to the metallic accents and lighting.

Similarly, plain floors were often covered with decorative carpeting like that made at Cranbrook, where the geometric design echoed the surrounding architectural features. Other rugs bore patterns suggesting Chinese or Navaho designs.

III-138. The floor design at the Kansas City Municipal Auditorium uses inset circles to replicate motifs on the ceiling.

III-139. The carpet design is a focal point in a Saarinen room at Cranbrook.

III-140. Deco theater carpeting that was sold in the 1930s was
clearly influenced by modernist European art.

IDIOMATIC ARCHITECTURAL FEATURES

As we have seen, ornamentation of all kinds was central to the Deco interior. In addition, there were certain idiomatic architectural elements that helped define the Deco style. Distinctive fireplaces and staircases were two such features.

Fireplaces

The fireplace, though no longer needed as a major heating unit for a room, nevertheless took a prominent position in Deco room design. And, like other elements of the décor the fireplace often became a focal point for original design. With newer technology allowing for a variety of materials, the fireplace became a decorative, charming, or dramatic statement that echoed material elements like metal or tile work, and architectural details, such as curves, steps, or triangles.

Eero Saarinen's 1929 fireplace for Cranbrook is an example of the imaginative use of materials, and the streamlined design favored by many other Deco designers. His fireplace, ornamented with his own bronze andirons, is made of a dull brown tile, with edgings of silver. Its shape is wide and horizontal. Its delicate edging and ornamentation in silver outlines the geometric shape, while contrasting with the andiron birds. With their long bodies and tails in a picturesque arch, they sit upon stepped pedestals familiar to Deco design. Such a complete design statement made the fireplace a central element in the room.

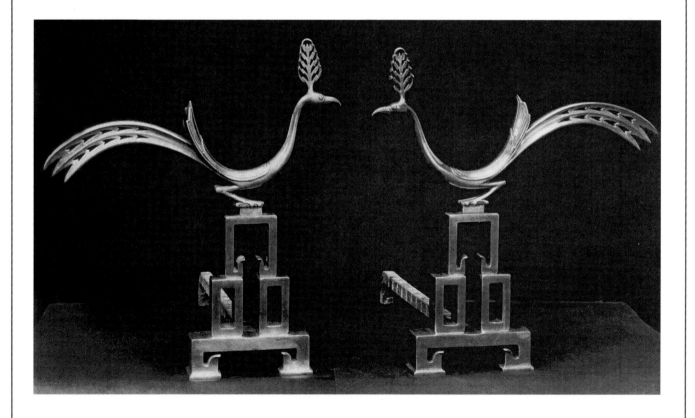

III-141 (above) & III-142 (opposite). Geometric design of Cranbrook's
tiled fireplace is contrasted with ornamental bronze bird andirons.

Typically Art Deco is the decorative steel fireplace, with matching mirror above; it was designed in the 1930s for a model room by General Electric. This fireplace has many Deco elements, the stepped lines, wavy stripe borders, and curves combined with angularity; all of these features appear in a highly reflective, bright and polished metallic surface that is complimented by the outline of the mirror above it.

The stepped fireplace of the Chanin Building is another Deco-oriented fireplace, with its repeated stepped outline ornamented with an octagonal centerpiece, and complex, decorative metal screen.

III-143. A fireplace from a 1930s General Electric model room has proportions and wavy parallel lines typical of the Deco era, as well as a characteristic stepped mirror shape.

III-144. The stepped firesplace of the Chanin Building in New York was in the 50th story theater's lobby. An ornate grillwork screen contrasts with geometric blocks of the fireplace design.

Staircases

Yet another element of Deco design that dramatically represented the vertical sweep and contrast of straight and curving lines was the staircase. Stairs became a focal point for many interiors. Whether open-faced, decoratively ornamented swoops (relating directly to their Art Nouveau ancestors), or cool geometric formations typical of Art Moderne, stairs in the Deco interior took a central place in the overall design.

Two European examples were influential in stair design. In Paris Jacques Doucet created a particularly jazzy 1930 version of the Deco staircase. In this charming and original example, the stair became a playful, linear design, closely related to abstract painting. In a less geometric, more flowing style, Pierre Ponsard's wrought iron balustrade also employed an imaginative design that suggested the formal elements of a landscape.

III-145 (right) and III-146 (above). Two well-known staircase designs of the French Deco era influenced American designers; one was a Mondrian-like stair by Jacques Doucet, and the other a Pierre Ponsard stair with an ornamental balustrade.

In the United States the staircase also became a focal point. Of course, the American Deco stair usually emphasized some sort of verticality. But the way this was achieved varied widely, and reflected the changing elements of Deco toward more streamlined design.

Eero Saarinen, in the stair he designed for Cranbrook, stressed the upward sweep of the steps by a repeated sharp-edged tile motif, with building-like railing projections on every other step. The slight curve of these rising images formed a contrast with the basic geometric design.

III-147. A tiled staircase from the Kingswood lobby at Cranbrook used slightly curved, repeated railing motif to contrast with strict geometry of the stair.

More reminiscent of the Art Moderne style of severe geometry, with its parallel horizontal stripes and angular, zigzag or reversal of direction, is the stairway designed for a Miami hotel. The bright, jazzy, upbeat coloring and lighting typify the exuberance of Miami Art Deco, and the continuing fascination with streamlining, bright lights, and décor suggesting a sense of movement.

III-148. A Deco staircase at the Kenmore Hotel in Miami features the lighted, streamlined, jazzy look that became popular in the 1930s.

The staircase, like other aspects of the Deco interior, was a setting for a mixture of materials. Typical of these mixed-media design elements was the elaborate staircase in the Chrysler Building that used a variety of materials, angles, and designs. Another is in the Cincinnati landmark hotel, the Netherlands Plaza (now the Hilton) with its combination of geometry and elaborate metalwork.

III-149. The Chrysler Building staircase, made of a mix of materials, contrasted zigzag design of its railing with circular motif above.

III-150. The staircase in the landmark Cincinnati Netherlands Plaza Hotel (now the Hlton) combines geometry with elaborately detailed ironwork.

The lighted stair was a popular idiom. Perhaps the most fantastic of such stairways, however, was the Kalamazoo City Hall stairway, boasting its own miniature lighted skyscraper. Here in a small city in the Midwest was a symbol of the great metropolis. The stair, with its lighted tower at the entrance, was itself fancifully ornamented with an eagle, while around it were contrasting architectural steps and elaborate grillwork.

III-151. One of the most striking staircases in American Deco is in Kalamazoo's City Hall, where a miniature lighted skyscraper ornaments the bottom of the structure.

III-152. Oakland's Paramount Theater has staircases to the mezzanine that combine many Deco idioms: elaborate metalwork, chrome railings, and a backdrop of illuminated glass that functions as false windows.

The extraordinary lobby of the Pautages Hotel in Los Angeles combines many of these elements in over-the-top Deco design—from stairs to ceiling.

III-153. The glamorous, highly decorated Pantages Theater in Los Angeles combines many Deco elements into a true fantasy decor—befitting a movie palace.

DECO FURNITURE

The enjoyments of mixed materials—and in particular fine woods—extended, as we know, to the brilliantly designed furniture of the Deco era. American Deco furniture, as in France, was created to complement and extend the Deco aesthetic of its surroundings. Combining various woods and other materials—from marble to glass—Deco furniture featured similar proportions, and geometric and natural motifs as the architecture around it. Shapes, like those of bookcases and even chair backs echoed the design of tall buildings, with pyramids and stepped designs. Typically Deco furniture combined the graceful curves and geometric angles so characteristic of the rooms it adorned.

American Deco furniture was primarily about fine wood, and the combining of different tones and grains. Most commonly used woods for furniture were mahogany and rosewood, elm and sycamore, and many fruitwoods. Exotic woods, including ebony, macassar, palisander, and satinwood were often used for detailing, in contrast with the very shiny polished surfaces of the main part of the furniture. A highly finished look was characteristic of the period, with many pieces covered with lacquer.

Ironwork with its decorative curlicues gave fire screens, table legs, and other parts of furniture an ornamental look. Glass, as in the Deco interior, was used for tabletops and mirrored surfaces, and in the many lighting fixtures and "mood" lamps that became popular. Fabric, with typically Deco patterns, covered chair seats and sofas. Today, American Deco furniture is highly prized, both for its design and for its extremely fine craftsmanship.

American Deco furnishings, now highly regarded by collectors, shared many characteristics with the French (as seen on pages xx). Some typical examples follow:

III-154. American Deco piano is made of Bird's Eye maple, mahogany, and brass; it was created in 1936 specifically for the opening of the Chrysler Building.

III-155. Vanity with mirror has dark outlines and drawer pulls that accentuate geometric pattern and curving edge.

III-156. Stepped "skyscraper" cabinet is made of birch and lacquer; it is one of many designs of the period based on urban building silhouettes.

III-157. Multi-colored chair is by Paul Frankl; it is influenced by Chinese, as well as geometric design.

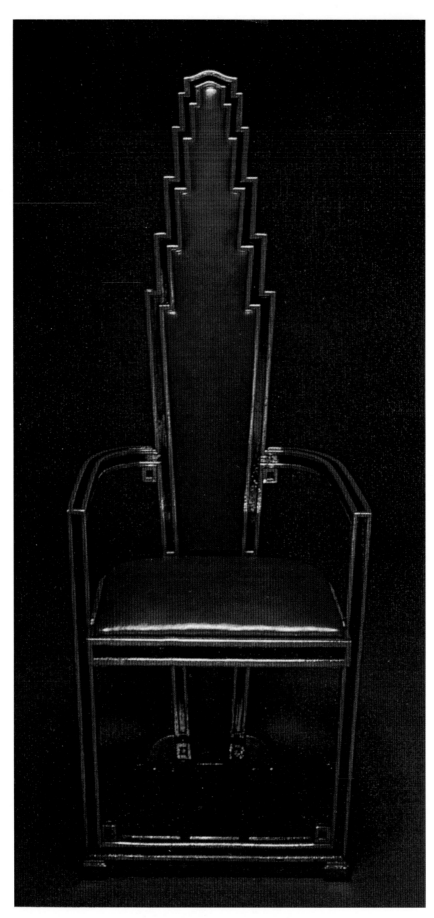

III-158. "Skyscraper" chair, like the cabinet on page 166 (III-156),
features a stepped outline with double stripes to accentuate its shape.

III-159. "Mood" lamp in Depression Green (actually white painted metal) was made by Frankart in 1929.

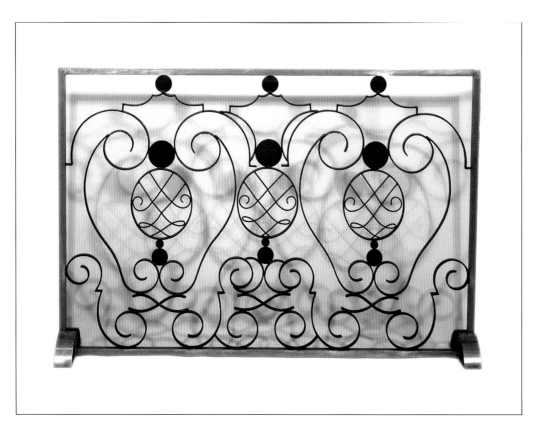

III-160. 1930s fire screen of wrought iron bears fanciful curlicues inside straight borders.

III-161. Mirrored side table has nickel and glass legs; it was made in the United States in the 1930s.

III-162. Typical Deco side table of 1930s America has graceful, curving, metal legs.

III-163. Fire screen was made c. 1935 in striking abstract design in bronze.

III-164. Glass stool with original leopard-skin upholstery typifies period's emphasis on exotic design and pattern.

PART IV

ART DECO RETURNS

Art Deco is back. While post-modernism has brought us a return to many historical styles (often used in an architectural mélange), Art Deco has, in many ways, made a comeback on its own. Beginning in about 1970, with the advent of preservationist groups in the United States and abroad, Deco buildings began to be given landmark status in many cities. There is new enthusiasm for both the architecture and furnishings in many parts of the world. (In 1960 London's magnificent Strand Hotel lobby was dismantled as "tacky;" today all that remains of its once spectacular Deco design is a basement railing. But the Victoria and Albert Museum has recently reconstructed this landmark lobby for an exhibition.)

The current climate for renovation rather than demolition is leading us to preserve buildings from the Deco era, with many architects and craftspeople recreating the original with painstaking care. Several of the following projects demonstrate the complex and elaborate renovation of landmark Deco buildings in the United States. In some examples of the adaptive reuse of old buildings, architects have preserved Deco elements while changing the use and orientation of the original. While such renovation is not always historically accurate, it has saved many Deco buildings from extinction.

But all Art Deco today is not a recreation of the past. On the contrary, many contemporary architects are turning to the Deco idiom because it fits so well into the styles and designs of today. The geometric cubistic grids, ornate grillwork, fine woods, elegant lighting, interplay of curve and straight lines, and above all, the emphasis once again on décor that is ornamental and decorative—these are just a few of the elements of Deco design that have resurfaced in today's architecture.

The projects that follow, ranging from the interiors of public buildings such as hotels and office towers and theaters to private homes and their furnishings, show the many ways in which the Deco and the contemporary have been merged into a new style.

IV-0. Molding design from the Wiltern Theater in Los Angeles

Public Buildings: Hotels, Office Towers, and Theaters

A Contemporary Hotel Lobby with Modern Deco Overtones

Stephen B. Jacobs of the Stephen B. Jacobs Group, P.C., New York City

One of New York's newest, most chic hotels is called Hotel Giraffe. Stephen Jacobs designed it in a Deco-Moderne style that is both sophisticated and inviting.

Decorated with warm, rich tones throughout, the interiors are filled with both large and small details suggested by the Moderne era, and with Deco-inspired furniture and objects. The public rooms, with their high ceilings and warm colors are particularly Deco-oriented.

The lobby, which is transformed into a piano bar in the evenings, is a deep-toned, cozy interior; its high ceiling is illuminated by starry lights set within a magenta-lighted geometric grid. There are dark wood stripes throughout, inset at several levels into the polished light wood paneling throughout the room, while the elevators are done with stripes of different woods and proportions. The windows echo the stripes and oblongs of the interior. As in so many Deco interiors, the geometry of stripes and squares is offset by curves; in this room the arch over the elevators, the round ceilings, the sinuous carpet edge, and the curving lines of the furniture serve that function. In addition, the carpet is ornamented with a complex geometric pattern, in similarly round and straight designs in matching warm tones.

A white-curtained meeting room in the penthouse has dramatic high ceilings where semi-circles at the edge of it and above the wood-clad fireplace pick up a similar design element of circles on the upholstery and on the back of the Deco chairs. Wall fixtures imitate the look of the thirties. In both rooms small objects, like the Deco-era cocktail shaker, add to the inviting Retro atmosphere.

IV-2. High-ceilinged penthouse meeting room has wood paneled fireplace and Deco lighting and objects.

IV-1. Warm-toned lobby/piano bar features grids on ceiling and windows, geometric Deco-style carpeting, and magenta lighting.

IV-3. Decorative curves in architecture and furniture contrast with
vertical columns and stripes, and geometric grid on ceiling.

A Converted Post Office With Deco Details

Tuck Hinton Architects, Nashville, Tennessee

Not long ago a grand historic post office in downtown Nashville was converted into the glamorous Frist Visual Arts Center. Originally built in 1934, the fine marble exterior was in Federal Classic style, but its interior was thoroughly Art Deco. As a post office it had become underused and out of date, but it was seen as a great site for adaptive reuse. Today it houses art and educational facilities, galleries, an auditorium, shops, and offices in a brilliant adaptation of the original Deco interior.

Tuck Hinton Architects undertook the renovation of the art center, focusing on the latest in curatorial technology and natural illumination, as well as on its historic design. New additions and entrances and renovations of the original interior were all part of this vast project.

A new corridor and gallery bring visitors directly into what was the original Deco main postal lobby. This huge area serves as the primary public space in the building, now a new clerestoried space filled with natural light. It is in this lobby, with its distinctive metal grid work, that the Deco details were carefully restored, while new Deco-inspired elements were added. Sections of the walls of the long corridor used by the post office were removed to create access to galleries and shops; green, beige, and black marble and terrazzo flooring and walls connect the original and new areas. End-grain wood block was salvaged from postal workrooms and reinstalled for gallery floors.

New aluminum accents were added to complement the existing metal grid that was a hallmark of the Deco interior. (The original grillwork was so stained by tobacco and coal smoke that it was thought to be bronze.) Lighting fixtures that recall the 1930s origins of the interior were installed the length of the ceiling. Galleries on the second floor are reached by prominent new staircases at each end of the lobby; railings and grills on the windows pay continuing homage to the Deco original.

This impressive reworking and reuse of a city's cultural heritage is one of many being undertaken across the nation. (The Frist Center for the Visual Arts is on the National Historic Register.) A number of these "saved" buildings were constructed in the 1930s, and like this example, refresh and renew the Deco idiom while adapting the building to modern use in a modern era.

IV-4. View of original Post Office lobby before renovation.

IV-5. Newly done entrance retains Deco look with tall arches and sun-like beams.

IV-6

IV-6 & IV-7. Renovated lobby emphasizes the Deco era grids and proportions; it now opens to galleries and shops.

IV-7

IV-8. Prominent new staircase has metal accents; original grids and lighting fixtures are retained.

Updated Deco Texas Movie Palace

David M. Schwarz / Architectural Services, Inc., Washington, D.C.

Movie theaters were among the prime examples of Art Deco in America. Many downtowns across the country still have a Deco movie house—often unused—but still featuring the faded elegance of a glamorous past. The preservation and updating of those that have survived the past half-century allows today's architects to combine past and present in new ways.

Architect David M. Schwarz of Washington and his associates undertook to bring a Deco movie palace in Fort Worth, Texas, into contemporary times without losing its fabled Deco appeal. Today's Sundance AMC Eleven Cinemas was originally built in the 1930s in a Deco style described as "a set for an imaginary Busby Berkeley musical."

The architects renovated and updated this glamorous site, leaving intact its Deco façade and vertical neon sign. Inside, shining metal sheathing, mirrors, and theatrical lighting were central to their design. The spectacular interior features a riveted metal, four-story lobby with a backlit skyline view made with etched glass panels. The riveted metal motif appears throughout the cinema complex. Surrounding this romantic scene is a nightscape of electric blue walls that dim and brighten with the use of a theatrical lighting system. Even the concession stand is sheathed in metal with Deco detailing, and its popcorn sign is written in appropriately Deco lettering.

Gleaming escalators add to the emphasis on shiny metal; they carry visitors to an upper lobby which is entered between reflective metal newel posts and an arched geometric "urban truss" reminiscent of a city bridge of the 1930s. Wall-sized mirrors given an added sense of space to the already grand lobby, while corridors leading to the eleven screening rooms are also lined with mirrors and etched glass tower designs. The tower theme is continued on the walls of each theater, and wall sconces provide subtle lighting. With its romantic urban theme and its emphasis on metal and glass, this theater complex recreates in a modern cinema the glamour of the movie palace of the 1930s.

IV-9. Exterior of old movie house has Deco façade and neon sign.

IV-10 (above) & IV-11 (following page). Entryway and sleek escalators feature gleaming detailing; four-story lobby has an interior of riveted metal.

IV-11

IV-12. Back-lit skyline view is made with etched glass panels.

IV-13. Decorative "urban truss" of shiny metal is reminiscent of 1930s bridge.

IV-14. Concession stand is sheathed in metal with Deco detailing.

IV-15. Theater interiors have tower theme, soft Deco lighting, and stepped silhouettes.

Combining "Futuristic" and Deco Design: A Corporation Headquarters

Mark Simon, FAIA and Jean E. Smajstrla, AIA of Centerbrook Architects, Centerbrook, Connecticut

The newly renovated interior of the corporate headquarters for a major corporate-benefits consulting firm is described by its architects at Centerbrook as "futuristic." This redone space certainly looks new and up-to-date. But the colorful interior, overlooking the Hudson River and New York City in Fort Lee, New Jersey, also bears a striking resemblance to Art Deco interiors of many decades ago.

In fact, the architects wanted to recall the past, not only in materials and design, but also in celebration of Fort Lee's famous Palisades Amusement Park, now long gone. With this hallowed and fun-filled past in mind, a number of design choices were made, including the use of materials popular in the Deco age, such as glass blocks, metal grids, neon lighting, Formica, and aluminum trim.

The offices and adjacent hallways were designed with backlit black grids and neon lighting in the halls, and the typically Deco combination of black Formica with aluminum coffers in the offices. There is a great deal of glass: brightly colored, neon-lit glass-block panels frame the entry doors off the lobby, while glass dividers separate work areas. Rectangular grids and dots (the signature motifs of the company) are repeated throughout the interior—on doors, ceilings, and wall screens. Porthole windows and geometric divisions also recall the Deco era. (And in reminiscence of the famous amusement park, glass dividers in the shapes of the roller coasters that once soared atop the Palisades flank the work-stations that are decorated with old photos of the park.) Deep, rich colors are used throughout.

By combining these many elements of the past with a contemporary and technologically updated use of space, this interior shows how Deco ideas and materials can be retrofitted into a contemporary style.

IV-16. Neon-lit glass block panels frame the entry doors off the lobby.

IV-17. Porthole windows and geometric divisions recall Deco era.

IV-18. Rectangular grids and dots (the company's motifs) are repeated throughout.

Geometric Patterns in the Humana Building, a Contemporary Louisville Office Tower

Michael Graves Architects, Princeton, New Jersey

Michael Graves began to incorporate Deco imagery into his designs for buildings (as well as household objects and accessories) in the 1970s, long before the style's current popularity. He was one of the first American architects to include Deco features in his post-modernist designs. Among his Deco oriented buildings were the Portland (Oregon) Public Services Building and. in 1985, the Humana Building in Louisville, Kentucky (shown here).

The design for the twenty-six story office tower for the Humana Company was chosen in an international competition and was the winner of numerous awards for architecture. It suggests skyscrapers of the Deco era, with its modified ziggurat-shaped topping, and its grand vertical entrance set amid repeated pillars.

The interior, designed by Graves/Warneke, includes much public space. The public loggia shows how Art Deco elements reappear in a modern form: there are alternating geometrical stripes and squares, stepped-back wall sections, and sleek metal detailing reminiscent of Machine Age design. The furniture, fabric design, metal railings, and bordered carpeting in the Humana Building are equally geometric in design. Although these details are drawn from the Art Deco era, the overall impression is of a modern interior, rather than a revival of a past style.

Graves's incorporation of past design idioms into a contemporary style is the very essence of post-modernism, while Art Deco, itself developing out of so many disparate artistic sources, seems the perfect component of such contemporary design.

IV-19. Exterior suggests skyscrapers of the 1930s, with its modified ziggurat topping and strongly vertical entrance.

IV-20. Contemporary interior uses Deco elements including geometric stripes and squares, stepped-back wall sections, and sleek metal railings.

IV-71. Architectural design is echoed in bordered floor carpeting and geometric furniture.

The Restoration and Updating of a Hartford Art Deco Theater and Concert Hall

Venturi, Scott Brown Associates, Philadelphia, Pennsylvania; in association with George Izenour

The renovation of Bushnell Memorial Hall in Hartford, Connecticut, included both the restoration of its Art Deco interior, originally completed in the 1920s, as well as many new elements designed to improve and update the venerable music hall. A 2300 seat multi-use theater, Bushnell Memorial Hall is Hartford's main venue for orchestra, opera, and popular music concerts.

The architectural firm of Venturi, Scott Brown and Associates, in association with George Izenour, a specialist in theater design, made a number of changes to improve seating, the orchestra pit, acoustics, and sight lines.

Of particular interest to Art Deco aficionados was the painstaking restoration of the interior decoration. The elaborate Deco ornamentation features long, repeated, brightly gilded strips with a complex arrangement of motifs: intersecting arches and stars, squares, stripes, and circles—all illuminated with Deco wall sconces. Each section of wall ornament continues onto a curved ceiling and then across the ceiling itself, until it reaches a giant celestial scene of the sun with parallel rays shining through clouds.

This ornamentation was painstakingly redone in order to recreate the gilded, jewel-like ambiance of the original Deco era, when theaters were seen as gloriously ornate, fanciful settings for an evening of enchantment.

IV-22. Elaborate renovation restored interior of hall to its gilded, jewel-like, Deco ambiance.

IV-23. Painstaking restoration of interior surfaces captures the original Art Deco ambiance.

Fantasy and Retro Design at a Tokyo Resort Hotel

Robert A.M. Stern Architects, New York, New York

The new Disney Ambassador Hotel, part of Japan's first large Disney resort, was designed by architect Robert A.M. Stern of New York to continue the Disney theme of fantasy and glamour. The architect chose to use an "art moderne" design for the hotel with many Deco-like features within. The interior looks back to an era when travel and movies were a romantic escape, and when the details of Deco design suggested that glamour and fantasy.

The many public rooms and hallways make use of that traditional Deco emphasis on circles and stripes and squares. The ceilings of these interiors are divided into large round patterns of light and design, while the walls are punctuated with vertical columns and stripes—some painted, some architectural. In the hallway, the same contrast in forms appears in the carpeting, which is ornamented with a typically Art Deco design of broken circles and squares.

The wedding chapel suggests architecture designed as fantasyland; details include the church-like leaded windows, arches, and a long center aisle. Retro features encompass a variety of small ornamental details that refer directly to the ornamentation of Art Deco buildings. Among them are curlicue metal grids at the entrance and along the sidewalls, typically 1930s leading in the windows, and metal wall sconces.

In creating this brand-new, but Retro-detailed, hotel so far from Art Deco's origins, the architect and designers suggest that the Deco style means glamour and fantasy no matter where it appears.

IV-24. Hotel in Tokyo recreates a fanciful version of the Deco era; corridor uses Deco design elements to elegant effect.

IV-25 (above), IV-26 & IV-27 (following page) Chapel has repeated
arches and Deco detailing to create fairy-tale atmosphere.

IV-26

Restoring a Cleveland Landmark: Severance Hall

David M. Schwarz/Architectural Services, Inc., Washington, D.C.

Severance Hall in Cleveland is one of the nation's most venerable buildings. The great sandstone and Indiana limestone hall in neoclassical style opened in 1931 and became the home of the Cleveland Orchestra. Its much-loved interior by the firm of Walker and Weeks was a heady mix of Art Deco, neoclassicism, and Egyptian Revival styles (a combination in itself indicative of the Deco era).

By 1958 the internationally famous orchestra found the hall too small and technologically old-fashioned. A new musical shell was inserted within the structure, covering up the famous organ, and eliminating many of the original architectural wonders of the interior.

Recently, an entirely different direction was undertaken both to renovate the historic structure to its original elegance, and to provide more space and modernize the facilities. In keeping with today's new emphasis on the preservation of historical architecture, extraordinary efforts were made to return the interior of Severance Hall to its former glory, from floral ceiling patterns to bas-reliefs and Deco lighting fixtures. David M. Schwarz/Architectural Services, Inc. undertook the task. By adding space for the newly exhumed organ, creating new public areas, and renovating the many architectural details that Walker and Weeks had originally included, the archi-

tects were able to create a more modern hall that nonetheless represents a distinctive architectural era.

The auditorium itself is now a glamorous, lacy interior; the cleaned or releafed aluminum filigree patterns on the walls and ceilings (said to have been based upon the design of the lace of Mrs. Severance's wedding dress) were restored. The curved walls, sloping ceilings, and open grillwork were also part of the successful acoustical plan for the hall's great orchestral and organ sound. Faux-Egyptian palm and fan shapes on the walls and many parallel stripes (including those of the newly installed organ) intermixed with leafy plant designs to brilliantly recreate the Deco style.

In the hallways decorative grills, marble surrounds, and Deco lighting fixtures were restored or recreated. Egyptian-style bas-reliefs in octagonal frames are set amid symmetrical designs in both gilt and ironwork. Even the coat check booth is a small Deco composition. Hallway colors echo those of the concert hall.

Despite these many historic renovations and recreations, Severance Hall is thoroughly up-to-date in technical terms, setting an example of how the great buildings of the past can be both preserved and modernized for the twenty-first century.

IV-28. Newly renovated Severance Hall is returned to its glamorous Deco-era past.

IV-29 & IV-30 (opposite). Walls and ceiling display lacy designs, faux-Egyptian shapes, and leaf patterns in aluminum filigree.

IV-31 & IV 32 (opposite). Hallways have decorative grills, marble surrounds, Egyptian bas-reliefs, and Deco lighting fixtures.

Interpreting Deco: An Updated Philadelphia Landmark

Venturi, Scott Brown, and Associates, Inc., Philadelphia, Pennsylvania

In the center of Philadelphia stands a landmark Art Deco tower called the Metropolitan. Built between 1926 and 1928, it still had many Deco features but needed a thorough renovation. The building had originally been constructed for the Armed Services Division of the Y.M.C.A.

The architectural firm of Venturi, Scott Brown, and Associates, Inc. undertook to return the interior of the building to a modernized Deco idiom. They created 120 newly designed apartments and some commercial space at street level. It was the lobby that retained most of the Deco elements.

And today no section of the building more clearly reflects the architects' desire to recreate a Deco sensibility than the lobby. Described by the architects as "a mix of original Art Deco elements and new design elements that interpret the Art Deco style," the lobby has many distinctive features. The original dark marble pilasters and carved door jambs have been retained, as has the 1928 gilt plaster frieze of sea horses and plants. But new to the interior is a stenciled wall pattern of typically Deco motifs (semi-circles, squares, dots) in shades of gray and mauve, with gold accents.

New Retro-furniture with rounded shapes and soft tones, as well as subdued lighting also recreate the past history of the Metropolitan. A repeated geometric wallpaper design interspersed with marble on the walls, a stylized Deco print, and a brass torchere (standing lamp, whose outline echoes the semi-circular wall pattern) completes the décor's interpretation of the past.

IV-33. Lobby design features marble and Deco-design wallpaper, rounded period furniture, and torchere lamp.

HOME INTERIORS

Home Designs Blending Past and Present

Alexander Gorlin Architects, New York City

The architecture of Alexander Gorlin harmoniously blends the modern and the classical, taking from each proportions and idioms that he fuses into his own personal style. In residences ranging from seaside villas to city lofts, he demonstrates his appreciation for stylistic details of the past, including those of the Art Deco era. Important to many of his designs are stairways—an element of design that often took center stage in the Deco interior. Shown here are three examples.

Gorlin's apartment design for a pre-war Manhattan duplex is typical of his enthusiasm for designs of the past set within modernist spaces. Here, within a double-height foyer, is a helix-shaped staircase reminiscent of the Deco era. Its curving shape and wrought iron and wood railing have the geometric patterning and proportions of Deco. They are echoed by—and contrasted with—the overhead lighting fixture and the adjacent small, elegant marble entry. Its formal geometry and rich colors, accented by black, are created with gold leaf and alabaster. The charm of this small vestibule suggests antiquity (and Deco's fusing of the exotic and historical), as its design plays off the squares and curves of the stairway.

In the Eclipse Townhouse, a villa designed for Seaside in Florida, Gorlin created a tall building based on a tripartite classical Italian palazzo. But in the interior he used large, vertical, contemporary spaces, with an open, modernist stair zigzagging around a central pier. The staircase is a central design element with its crisp, streamlined Deco-like parallel stripes and angles. Its stairwell serves as a skylight too.

In another home in Seaside, his Ruskin Place Townhouse, Gorlin also uses stairs as the major design element of the interior. In this room an encased, winding, white stairway, ornamented with stark black railings and a tall pole, makes a dramatic statement. Its curvy shape contrasts with the vertical pillar opposite, and with the geometrically divided space next to it. Another stepped element decorates the ceiling. In all of these rooms the staircase adds interest and ornamentation, much as it did in many Deco interiors.

IV-34 (top) & IV-35. In a Manhattan duplex, wrought iron and wood stair and geometric alcove combine classical and Deco idioms.

IV-36. In a Seaside townhouse the streamlined staircase takes center stage.

IV-37. Curving stair in another Seaside villa contrasts with geometric and stepped architectural elements.

Bold Contemporary Pied-a-Terre with Deco Design and Furniture

Charles Gwathmey of Gwathmey/Siegel Architects, New York City

Turning an ordinary Manhattan two-bedroom pied-a-terre into a serene but chic architectural statement was recently the task of New York architect Charles Gwathmey of Gwathmey/ Siegel Architects. The solution included gutting the original apartment and combining bold contemporary spaces and formal invention with Deco era design and furniture.

Although it has only 2000 square feet of area, the apartment nevertheless creates a spacious environment with a variety of ceiling heights and architectural forms. There are many rounded lines, such as the large canted stainless steel column, and floor and ceiling curves. The varied ceilings (originally quite low) now have occasional plaster canopies, and sloping and curving sections, creating a more vertical space. A new five-sided bay window configuration gives the apartment dramatic views of the city, and is just one of many choices made to lighten the apartment.

A suggestion of Cubist and Deco design appears in the gridded beech and cherry paneling that covers many walls and built-in cabinets, as well as in the angled walls themselves. Like many interiors in the 1930s, the use of different woods is a major visual element with a light beech (with occasional deep-toned cherry wood) on the walls, and the use of cherry or pale maple for most of the flooring. A variety of geometric rectangles and squares on the cabinets plays off the curving architectural spaces. The exterior walls of the guest room/ study are white glass, while the interior of the room is lined with grids—some of wood and some made of suede panels.

Additional Art Deco notes are created by the furniture. Much of it is in the style of the great French Deco-era designer Jacques-Emile Ruhlmann, with some pieces made to order for the apartment from original designs by Ruhlmann. Luxurious patterned fabrics and textures create a sumptuous old-world quality, which contrasts—as in many Deco-oriented interiors—with the rigorous geometric motifs on the architectural surfaces.

IV-38. Large, canted, stainless steel column and circular ceiling canopies are featured in living room.

IV-39 & IV-40 (following page). Curving furniture designs suggestive of Deco era contrast with geometric architecture and shelving.

IV-41. The combination of geometric lines and forms with curving furniture is a nod to Deco Design.

Curving furniture designs suggestive of Deco era contrast with geometric architecture and shelving.

A Large Apartment Is Patterned on Deco Design

Richard Mervis, Designer, New York City

Today's interior designers frequently focus on the complexity of pattern in the Deco style. During the height of the Deco era, interiors featured many simultaneous patterns, both in architectural detail, such as metalwork and glass, and in elements of interior design, including coverings for floors, walls, and furniture. Artwork and elaborate lighting fixtures added to the mix. Carpet patterns and other textiles often had contrasting designs. As we have seen, many of these patterns were geometric, while others symbolized elements of nature. Images suggesting machinery and speed were also common.

Richard Mervis, an interior designer in New York, has recreated the ambiance of the Deco age through pattern in several apartments. In one he used both furniture and artwork (posters) to set the Deco stage. This Art Deco-inspired apartment on New York's Upper East Side incorporates stylistic Deco details in a large (6000 square feet) post-war apartment space.

The apartment features a variety of patterns in the sitting room, where chocolate brown walls provide a warm background. Deco-patterned fabric (from Clarence House) covers one chair and pillow with a forceful geometric design. The furniture, a marble-topped desk, end table, and lacquered coffee table, all designed to fit the updated Deco setting by Mervis himself, is a combination of opposites: curves and straight lines, soft leather and shiny marble. The eye-catching poster (though, like the building, post-war), emphasizes speed with typically machine-age, diagonal speed stripes stretching behind the motorcycle and racing car.

The dining room is lined with sycamore and bronze mirrors. Its floor is black and gold marble with inlaid squares of botticini marble. Mervis also designed the silver-leaf and lacquer dining table. Checkerboard fabric on the chairs echoes the (larger squares of the floor design. In this apartment, a variety of patterns, textures, and shapes create a Deco ambiance that nonetheless feels contemporary.

IV-42. Variety of patterns and textures and machine-age poster create Deco-like ambiance.

IV-43. Checkerboard chair coverings replicate larger squares of flooring.

Palm Desert Residence Reimagines Deco Era

Sally Sirkin Lewis, Inglewood, California

In a recent, eye-catching interior design, Sally Sirkin Lewis brings the Deco era to life with a combination of 1930s inspiration and contemporary sophistication. Both an interior and furniture designer, Lewis admires the combination of simplicity and luxuriousness found in Deco period rooms.

In the living room of this residence, she uses a balance of scale, contrasting materials, and vertical elements to create the Deco ambiance. (She comments that the angular lines and repetitive shapes also recall the principles of the Bauhaus.) Lewis designed the lacquered walls, the black leather, the tête-à-tête sofa, the steel and glass table, the curved lounge chairs, and the Art Deco armchair—all of which add to what she describes as " the luxurious simplicity " of the Art Deco interior. A 1930s Alliot granite panther sculpture on the table completes the interior's homage to the Deco era.

The home office of the same residence has tall ebony-lacquered doors with steam-lined hardware. Texture is emphasized with hemp wall covering, boucle fabric upholstery, and polished stainless steel. Furniture echoes the Deco theme: an articulated polished chrome table lamp with ivory details, and a limestone polar bear sculpture date to the 1930s, while contemporary furnishings, including a table with macassar ebony veneer and lounge chairs with stainless steel insets were designed recently in a similar period style. On the wall is a tapestry, also from the 1930s, by Arshile Gorky.

In the master bedroom a brushed stainless steel fireplace mantel and mesh steel curtains are complemented by a steel and glass table. Doors are wrapped in hemp. Contemporary art (by David Simpson) is aligned with a 1930s limestone maquette for a bronze sculpture from France of the 1930s.

IV-44. Living room combines Deco-influenced furniture designed by Lewis with careful composition of scale, materials, and vertical elements.

IV-45. Home office features tall ebony-lacquered doors with streamlined hardware, combination of textures and materials, and tapestry from the 1930s by Arshile Gorky.

IV-46. Brushed stainless steel fireplace and steel and glass table are centerpieces of master bedroom's minimalist, Deco-oriented design.

In another example, this one a pied-à-terre in Sarasota, Florida, Lewis designed both the interior and the furniture, creating the "visual luxury" that she associates with the Deco period, including designing the furniture. Strong geometric design of the entry contrasts circles and verticals. Minimalist furnishings are described as counterpoints to the elegant materials and surfaces: the floors are of quarter-sawn maple, the chandelier is in ash veneer, the Mushroom table is of polished stainless steel.

And in another entryway, in a residence in Bangkok, Lewis used a glamorous staircase to provide drama. The great curving stairway is surrounded by large-scale artworks and mirrors (to create a sense of space), upholstered walls, tall, ebony lacquered doors, and large black marble tiles. Lewis comments that "the 'editing'" of interior space was a skill used by Art Deco period room designers."

IV-47. Entryway in Sarasota residence uses contrasting geometric design and a variety of textures and materials to create elegant interior.

IV-48. Large, curving staircase, surrounded by mirrors and artwork, creates dramatic entrance for this Bangkok residence.

ARTISTS AND ARTISANS
RECREATING THE STYLE

Today's Furniture and Fabric Designs in Updated Deco Style

Sally Sirkin Lewis for J. Robert Scott, Inc., Inglewood, California

In keeping with the enthusiasm for Deco design in today's interiors, some interior designers are creating furniture and fabric as well. Sally Sirkin Lewis has designed and produced a number of such pieces, which recall the sleek elegance of the Deco era.

IV-49. "Essex" settee

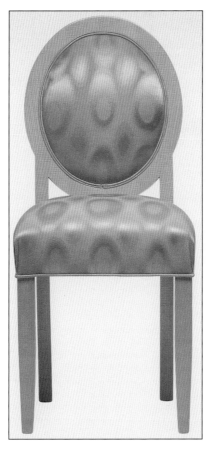

IV-50. Art Deco "Opera Chair"

IV-51. "Cloud" Chest

IV-52. "Normandie" Coffee Table

IV-53. "Deanna" Chair

IV-54. "Athena" Chandelier

IV-55. "Snail" Table

IV-56. "Lithic" Floor Lamp

IV-57. "Odete" Sconce

IV-58. "Les Pyramides" (Fabric)

IV-59. "Fleur Deco" (Fabric)

Deco Details in a Contemporary Home

Ted Montgomery of GroundSwell Architects, Charlotte, Vermont

Much of what we think of as the Art Deco interior is a compilation of details—certain types of fireplace, for example, or a certain use of grillwork, or 1930s-style furniture, or a glass brick wall. It is often these aspects of the style that are resurfacing today, even when placed in an otherwise contemporary setting.

Ted Montgomery of GroundSwell Architects has used just such a collection of details in his own Vermont home. His wood-burning copper fireplace is a box-like structure (with its own catalytic burning insert and knobs for clothes drying), ornamented with a striking, shiny metal and glass stovepipe and iron detail work, suggesting the Deco emphasis on the fireplace itself, as well as on the use of ornamental metal and glass.

His staircase has a decorative, curving railing made of copper tubing, sculpted from common plumbing parts, lacquered and set with the parallel lines and sweeps of the Deco era, but with a hint of anarchy in its vertical pieces. The railing design is balanced by—and contrasted with—a tall standing lamp, also of metal, which has three branching arms surrounded by flower-like shades.

A table by the architect also recalls the Deco period. This circular piece of furniture features decorative legs, whose wooden lengths are cut in parallel undulating curves, a wave-like design borrowed from the past. Details like these, set in an otherwise contemporary setting are another example of how Deco design can be integrated into an up-to-date home.

IV-60. Fireplace with copper and glass stovepipe; the combination of ornamental metal and glass also typified the Deco era, as well as much of today's design.

IV-61. Ornamental, curving copper-tubing railing complements standing lamp with flower-like shades.

IV-62. Table created by the architect features decorative legs with parallel, undulating curves.

IV-63. Mixing free-form with Deco-oriented design, architect created original, vibrant living room.

Pictorial Walls and Ceilings: Deco-Style Murals Return

EverGreene Painting Studios, Inc., New York City

Among the most decorative features of Art Deco is surely the use of pictorial walls and ceilings—those murals, trompe l'oeil designs, mosaics, frescoes, and ornamental patterns that bring color and imagery to the Deco interior. No other element so clearly indicates the integration of art and architecture in the Deco era. And the imagery chosen for those walls and ceilings has traditionally carried symbolic messages that convey the very heart of the Deco idiom: the glamour, the burgeoning plants, the goddesses, the emphasis on speed and motion, the inviting warmth of the sun.

EverGreene Painting Studios have become the leading creators of murals and other interior decoration in the Deco style. Their artists both restore original works in old buildings and create original designs that bring the Deco idiom to new life. The vast number of their projects, including dozens of historic theaters and concert halls (including Severance Hall, seen in these pages), renovated churches, capitol buildings, and private homes, points to the ongoing fascination with "built-in" art. A sampling of their original art demonstrates their use of the Deco style, some designed by outside decorators, and others by their own artists.

Murals were frequent additions to Deco public rooms. Today, Essex House in New York features a mural by EverGreene Studios. A beaming sun shines upon a scene of glamorous goddesses dressed in the classical style and pictured in symbolic poses. Like much Deco art in Europe and America in the 1930s, this design was created with the glazing of various metal leafs including copper, aluminum, silver, platinum, and gold. The effect created is of a trompe l'oeil bas-relief.

A large oval for a domed ceiling at Harrah's Casino in Joliet, Illinois, is another example of the continuing interest in the Deco style. (The design was by Dougall Design Associates.) The choice of color—warm reds and pinks—and intertwined flower and natural forms all suggest a modern version of Deco era.

Another casino mural, this one at the New York, New York Hotel/Casino in Las Vegas, includes imagery reflecting the history of the city's landmark buildings and bustling streetscape. The "News Building" section (shown here) features Deco-like rays of sunlight shining through clouds and steam, as well as stylized figures of the thirties.

A mural in a private residence was painted directly onto the stained wood folding doors of the media cabinet wall. The leafy treetops were gilded with pieces of gold leaf and the sky was leafed with aluminum. The ground, trees, and figures were lightly glazed so that the original sycamore wood pattern could be seen underneath. (The design was by Allene Simmons Interior Design, Inc.)

The Flynn Theater in Burlington, Vermont was elegantly ornamented with Deco-style murals and decorations in a recent renovation. The flower and geometric motifs, and the vibrant colors chosen give this attractive interior a jewel-like elegance.

And perhaps the most Deco-like of all was the imagery created for the perfume counter of the Dayton Hudson Department Store in Chicago. This dashing scene—featuring the ubiquitous leaping gazelles and dancing goddess in a moonlit, wind-blown night—is a thoroughly Deco creation, though it was designed recently. The image was etched into glass and then gilded from behind with gold, platinum, and silver leaf (techniques familiar in the past). The dark background was created by smoking the glass with a kerosene lamp.

IV-64. Mural at Essex House in New York City combines symbolic female figures and motifs of nature.

IV-65. Domed ceiling art at Harrah's Casino in Joliet, Illinois, recalls Deco design with swirling patterns and rich color. The inset shows the design studio.

IV-66. Las Vegas hotel/casino mural has New York City subject.

IV-67. Painting of trees covers cabinet's folding doors in a private home.

IV-68. Flynn Theater in Burlington, Vermont, is elegantly decorated with geometric and flower patterns.

IV-69. Department store mural has a mixture of plain and stained glass,
geometric grid, and fanciful images of woman and deer in motion.

Exceptional Glass Design Returns

David Wilson, South New Berlin, New York

The use of decorative glass was, of course, central to the Art Deco style. Stained, opaque, or etched glass, neon-lighted glass, mirrors, and glass combined with metal design, were all major aspects of the interiors of that era. Today, glass has again become a beautiful, as well as functional, element of contemporary design, and certain uses of it in modern buildings clearly reminds us of the important place it held in the Deco interior.

One of the leading contemporary glassmakers in the country, David Wilson of South New Berlin, New York, is frequently called upon to integrate glass design and architecture. His projects range from religious buildings, airports, medical centers, and major public buildings, to private residences. Wilson tries to work with the design sensibility of each project he undertakes, integrating glass with architectural details and overall style—sometimes in the Art Deco idiom.

Particularly bringing to mind the geometric designs and verticality favored by Deco architecture is Wilson's vast, elegant window for the Stamford, Connecticut, Courthouse. Here combinations of delicately colored and etched glass panes are set in a tall and elegant rectangle; within each interior section a variety of geometric patterns interact with the squares-within-squares of the design.

Another example that recalls the Deco emphasis on glass design is the curving glass screen that Wilson created for Corning Glass Incorporated. Known as the "Wavewall Project," this elegant screen combines the undulating curves and periodic verticals so typical of the Deco era, with small geometric patterns within each section. But its use in the expansive Corning interior seems thoroughly contemporary.

Today's new airport buildings continue to use elements of art and architecture to capture the "romance" of flight, much as they did when airplane traffic first became popular. Several airports feature Wilson's glass elements, including JFK Airport in New York, where his geometric patterned grid, with its combination of stained and clear glass creates a sense of movement and depth.

And a dramatic element of the architecture of the Syracuse Airport is Wilson's "Flight Canopy," an almost Cubist-looking, three-dimensional glass design of angles and curves that captures the emphasis on motion, speed, and flight that characterized so much Deco design of the 1930s.

IV-70

IV-70 (opposite) & IV-71 (above). Stamford, Connecticut,
Courthouse windows feature geometric patterns.

IV-72 (above) & IV-73. "Wavewall Project" for Corning Glass combines undulating curves and contrasting verticals.

IV-74. Window at Kennedy Airport has a mixture of plain and stained glass, as well as a geometric grid.

IV-75. Design of window at Syracuse Airport symbolizes motion, speed, and flight itself.

Deco-Oriented Metal Design of Today

Joel Schwartz's Forge and Metalworks, Inc., Deansboro, New York

Certainly one of the most noticeable elements of the Deco interior is metalwork, from lacy grills to dramatic curving railings. Many architects and designers today are using metal to ornament and highlight their interiors in much the same way. They frequently turn to Joel Schwartz to create metalwork for them, whether for renovating historic building interiors, or for completely new designs.

Schwartz, who has shown with his varied designs that metalwork can be a central aspect of a room, has created architectural and decorative elements for all kinds of venues, including the inside and outside of private homes and the updated Deco interior of Rockefeller Center in New York. He notes that his work "functions within, enhances, and complements the environment…by the sensitive application of traditional blacksmithing and modern metal fabrication techniques."

As we have seen, staircases and their decorative railings have long been a central feature of the Deco interior. Examples of Schwartz's sensitivity to the Deco design era include a series of balustrades: (1) a stair balustrade with gilded details for a private home in Harrison, New York featuring geometric repeating patterns and curlicues; (2) a stair balustrade for a New York City building with a decorative design of bronze detailing in a repeated Deco-style ornamental pattern; (3) a Rockefeller Center interior stair balustrade made of forged steel leaf work, Monel, Cupronickel, and stainless steel in a complex pattern of leaves and growth; and (4) a balustrade for a Connecticut site that intersperses delicate filigree work with geometric accents for a sweeping curved staircase.

In each of these examples, the metalwork element brings to the interior the kind of vibrant flourish that so often characterized the Deco interior. As much contemporary architecture begins to leave behind the minimalism of modern design, metal ornamentation is being given its most prominent role since the 1930s.

IV-76. A stair balustrade for a private home has Deco-like patterns.

IV-77. Repeated ornamental pattern decorates handrail in New York City apartment building.

IV-78. Rockefeller Center stair balustrade is made of several metals and has pattern of leaves and growth.

IV-79. Connecticut residence has elegant stair with complex filigree work.

THE ARCHITECTS,
DESIGNERS,
AND ARTISTS

EverGreene Painting Studios
450 West 31 Street
New York, New York 10001
(212) 244-2800

Alexander Gorlin Architects
137 Varick Street, 5th floor
New York, New York 10013
(212) 229-1199

Michael Graves and Associates
341 Nassau Street
Princeton, N.J. 08540
(609) 924-1795

Gwathmey, Siegel and Associates Architects
475 Tenth Avenue
New York, New York 10018
(212) 947-1240

Tuck Hinton Architects P.L.C.
410 Elm Street
Nashville, Tennessee 37203-4220
(615) 254-4100

Stephen B. Jacobs
The Stephen B. Jacobs Group, P.C.
677 Fifth Avenue
New York, New York 10022
(212) 421-3712

Sally Sirkin Lewis
J. Robert Scott, Inc.
500 North Oak Street
Inglewood, California 90302
(310) 680-4300

Richard Mervis Design, Inc.
654 Madison Avenue
New York, New York 10021
(212) 371-6363

Ted Montgomery
GroundSwell Architects
477 Ten Stones Circle
Charlotte, Vermont 05445
(802) 425-7717

Rothzeid, Kaiserman, Thomson & Bee (R.K.T&B.)
150 West 22nd Street
New York, New York 10011
(212) 807-9500

Joel Schwartz
Schwartz's Forge & Metalworks, Inc.
2695 Route 315 P.O. Box 205
Deansboro, New York 13328
(315) 841-4477

David M. Schwarz/ Architectural Services, Inc.
1707 L Street N.W. Suite 400
Washington, D.C. 20036
(202) 862-0777

Mark Simon, FAIA and Jean E. Smajstrla, AIA
Centerbrook Architects
67 Main Street P.O. Box 955
Centerbrook, Connecticut 06409-0955
(860) 767-0175

Robert A.M. Stern Architects
460 West 34th Street
New York, New York 10001
(212) 967-5100

Venturi, Scott Brown and Associates, Inc.
4236 Main Street
Philadelphia, Pennsylvania 19127-1696
(215) 387-0400

David Wilson Design
RD 2, Box 121A
South New Berlin, New York 13843
(607) 334-3015

PICTURE CREDITS

Many of the pictures included in this book come from periodicals of the Art Deco era, including: *Art et Décoration*, 1925–; *Art et Industrie*, 1925-1935; *Arts Decoration Magazine*, 1930s; *L'Art Vivant*, 1925-35; *The Spur Magazine*, 1920s; *Mobilier et Décoration*, 1925-30; *Metalcraft Magazine*, 1930s; *Illustration*, 1930s; *The Architect and the Engineer*, 1930s; and *Pleasure Magazine*, 1930s. I am grateful to several private collections for the use of images in this book. Contemporary photos, when not otherwise credited, are by the author. Some images are from the New York Public Library Picture Collection. I would particularly like to thank Maison Gerard in New York, The Cranbrook Archives, and the Corning Museum for their invaluable help. The contemporary architects and artists included made Part IV of this book possible; their addresses appear separately. In addition I would like to thank the following people and organizations for so graciously providing me with pictures for this book:

Front cover: Top left and top right: Photographs by E.H. D./J.R.; bottom right: Courtesy of Hilton Hotel, Cincinnati; bottom left:: *Illustration*, 1930. **Endsheets:** Courtesy David M. Schwarz/Architectural Services, Inc., Washington, D.C. **Title page:** Roxy Theater, Rockefeller Center, New York, NY; **Copyright page:** St. George's Hotel, Brooklyn, NY; **Back cover:** Shell Building, *The Architect and Engineer*, 1930.

Part I: Courtesy of Split Personality, Leah Roland: I-4; Private Collections: I-12, I-13, I-14; *L'Art Vivant*, 1925: I-16; Bauhaus Archive: I-25; Courtesy of Roman Bronze Works, I-32; Courtesy of Maison Gerard, New York: I-8, I-11, I-55, I-56, I-59, I-61, I-63, I-64, I-68; Courtesy of Maison Gerard, New York, photos by Robert Levin: I-36, I-58, I-62, I-65, I-66, I-67, I-69, I-70, I-71, I-73; Courtesy of Maison Gerard, New York, photo by David Zadeh: I-60; Courtesy of the Mexican Information Agency: I-38; Courtesy of the Egyptian Information Agency: I-42; all others: New York Public Library Picture Collection, collection of the author, and private collections.

Part II: Courtesy Unity Temple Restoration Foundation: II-5; Courtesy Illinois Historic Preservation Society, the Dana-Thomas House: II-6; Courtesy Hirschl and Adler Galleries, New York: II-7, II-9; Courtesy Modernism Fine Arts, New York: II-8; Courtesy of Roman Bronze Works: II-10. II-11, II-12; Courtesy of Island Outpost, Miami, photo by Cookie Kinkead: II-19; Courtesy of Maison Gerard, New York, photo by Robert Levin: II-20.

Part III: Courtesy of Cranbrook Archives: III-1, III-56, III-57, III-69, III-139, III-142, III-147; Photographs by E.H. D./J.R.: III-3, III-9, III-16, III-23, III-27, III-29, III-46, III-73, III-74, III-79, III-90, III-93, III-98, III-99, III-102, III-115, III-118, III-133, III-134, III-135, III-136, III-137, III-153;Courtesy of R.K.T.& B. Architects: III-10, III-17, III-19,

III-22, III-88, III-89; Courtesy of Hilton Hotel, Cincinnati: III-21, III-37; III-77, III-117; Courtesy of Roman Bronze Works: III-30, III-31, III-33, III-34, III-35, III-36, III-38, III-125, III-126; Courtesy of the National Sculpture Society: III-40; *The Dance Magazine of Stage and Screen*, 1925: III-41; *Pleasure Magazine*, 1937: III-48; Courtesy of Rob Mathewson, photographer: III-58, III-87, III-119, III-149; Courtesy of the Arizona Biltmore Hotel and Spa: III-53; Illinois Historic Preservation Society, the Dana-Thomas House: III 54 & 55; Courtesy of Saint Bartholomew's Church, New York: III-59, III-60; "Arts Decoration Magazine"1937: III-61; Courtesy of Corning Museum of Glass, Gift of Corning Glass Works: III-66, III-67; Courtesy of Corning Museum of Glass, gift of Benjamin D. Bernstein: III-82; Courtesy of Lost City Arts, New York: III-80, III-155; *Metalcraft Magazine*, 1930: III-81, III-110; *Architecture Magazine*, 1930: III-91; *American Architect*, 1929, 1934: III-95, III-127; Photo by Helga Photo Studios, by courtesy of the magazine *Antiques*: III-120; Courtesy of Catalina Island Museum: III-122; *The Spur Magazine*, 1928: III-123; Courtesy The Library of Congress: III-124; *Illustration*, 1930: III-145; Courtesy Best Western-Kenmore Miami: III-148; Courtesy Hilton Hotel, Cincinnati: III-150; Collection of Carol Conn and Walter Maibaum: III-154; Courtesy Skyscraper/ Deco Deluxe, New York: III-160, III-161, III-162, III-163, III-164.

Part IV. Courtesy Stephen B. Jacobs Group, P.C. New York: IV-1, IV-2, IV-3; Courtesy Tuck Hinton Architects, Nashville, Tennessee: IV-4, IV-5, IV-6, IV-7, IV-8; Courtesy David M. Schwarz/Architectural Services, Inc., Washington, D.C.: IV-9, IV-10, IV-11, IV-12, IV-13, IV-14, IV-15, IV-28, IV-29, IV-30, IV-31, IV-32; Courtesy Mark Simon, FAIA and Jean Smajstrla, Centerbrook Architects, Centerbrook, Connecticut, Photos by Jeff Goldberg/Esto: IV-16, IV-17, IV-18; Courtesy Michael Graves and Associates, Princeton, New Jersey, Photos by Paschall/Taylor: IV-19, IV-20, IV-21; Courtesy Venturi, Scott Brown and Associates, Philadelphia, Pennsylvania, Photos by Tom Bernard: IV-22, IV-23, IV-33; Courtesy Robert A.M. Stern Architects, New York, Photos by Peter Aaron/Esto: IV-24, IV-25, IV-26, IV-27; Courtesy Alexander Gorlin Architects, New York: IV-34, IV-35, IV-36, IV-37; Courtesy Gwathmey/ Siegel and Associates, Architects, New York: IV-38, IV-39, IV-40, IV-41; Richard Mervis, Design, Inc., New York: IV-42, IV-43; Sally Sirkin Lewis, Inglewood, California: IV-44, IV-45, IV-46, IV-47, IV-48; J. Robert Scott, Inglewood, California: IV-49, IV-50, IV-51, IV-52, IV-53, IV-54, IV-55, IV-56, IV-57, IV-58, IV-59; Ted Montgomery, GroundSwell Architects, Charlotte, Vermont: IV-60, IV-61, IV-62, IV-63; EverGreene Painting Studios, Inc., New York: IV-64, IV-65, IV-66, IV-67, IV-68, IV-69; David Wilson Design, S. New Berlin, New York: IV-70, IV-71, IV-72, IV-73, IV-74, IV-75; Schwartz's Forge and Metalworks, Inc., Deansboro, New York: IV-76, IV-77 (Morgancloglu Architects), IV-78 (Gensler and Associates, Architects).